how to be
better at....

motivating
people

THE INDUSTRIAL SOCIETY

The Industrial Society stands for changing people's lives. In nearly eighty years of business, the Society has a unique record of transforming organisations by unlocking the potential of their people, bringing unswerving commitment to best practice and tempered by a mission to listen and learn from experience.

The Industrial Society's clear vision of ethics, excellence and learning at work has never been more important. Over 10,000 organisations, including most of the companies that are household names, benefit from corporate Society membership.

The Society works with these, and non-member organisations, in a variety of ways – consultancy, management and skills training, in-house and public courses, information services and multi-media publishing. All this with the single vision – to unlock the potential of people and organisations by promoting ethical standards, excellence and learning at work.

If you would like to know more about the Industrial Society please contact us.

The Industrial Society
48 Bryanston Square
London
W1H 7LN
Telephone 0171 262 2401

The Industrial Society is a Registered Charity No. 290003

how to be
better at....

motivating
people

John Allan

KOGAN PAGE   The Industrial Society

YOURS TO HAVE AND TO HOLD
BUT NOT TO COPY

First published in 1996, reprinted 1997 (twice)

Apart from any fair dealing for the purposes of research or private study, or criticism or review, as permitted under the Copyright, Designs and Patents Act, 1988, this publication may only be reproduced, stored or transmitted, in any form or by any means, with the prior permission in writing of the publishers, or in the case of reprographic reproduction in accordance with the terms and licences issued by the CLA. Enquiries concerning reproduction outside those term should be sent to the publishers at the undermentioned address:

Kogan Page Limited
120 Pentonville Road
London N1 9JN

© John Allan,1996

The right of John Allan to be identified as author of this work has been asserted by him in accordance with the Copyright, Design and Patents Act 1988.

British Library Cataloguing in Publication Data
A CIP record for this book is available from the British Library.
ISBN   0 7494 1913 X

Typeset by Photoprint, Torquay, Devon
Printed in England by Clays Ltd, St Ives plc

CONTENTS

PREFACE

The theory in this book has been illustrated by means of real-life examples. Most of these examples are from my own experience. Others have been told to me. In all cases names and environments have been changed to avoid identification of the individuals involved – but all the examples really happened!

The first two chapters set out the basic theory of motivation and these should be read first.

At the end of each chapter there are a few questions to enable you to check that you have understood the chapter.

HOW TO BE A BETTER ... SERIES

Whether you are in a management position or aspiring to one, you are no doubt aware of the increasing need for self-improvement across a wide range of skills.

In recognition of this and sharing their commitment to management development at all levels, Kogan Page and the Industrial Society have joined forces to publish the How to be a Better ... series.

Designed specifically with your needs in mind, the series covers all the core skills you need to make your mark as a high-performing and effective manager.

Enhanced by mini case studies and step-by-step guidance, the books in the series are written by acknowledged experts who impart their advice in a practical way which encourages effective action.

Now you can bring your management skills up to scratch *and* give your career prospects a boost with the How to be a Better ... series!

Titles available are:

How to be Better at Giving Presentations
How to be a Better Problem Solver
How to be a Better Interviewer
How to be a Better Teambuilder
How to be Better at Motivating People
How to be a Better Decision Maker

Forthcoming titles are:

How to be a Better Negotiator
How to be a Better Project Manager
How to be a Better Creative Thinker
How to be a Better Communicator

Available from all good booksellers. For further information on the series, please contact:

Kogan Page, 120 Pentonville Road, London N1 9JN
Tel: 0171 278 0433   Fax: 0171 837 6348

1

WHAT'S IN IT FOR ME?

You want to be a successful manager, and you feel that motivating people has something to do with success. Would you have picked up this book if that were not so?

Everyone needs to motivate others, and we all do it, whether we realise it or not. Babies motivate parents – they stop crying when picked up! Parents motivate their children to work hard at school. I try to motivate the bored bank clerk by smiling at her (it's amazing how many people smile back!)

So – motivation is natural. Except, it seems, in management. Some of the earliest management studies were on how to motivate people to work harder.[1] Of course managers had always known how to make people work harder by threats: 'If this isn't finished by tonight you're sacked' has always been a great motivator. This is negative motivation. It worked when there was high unemployment. After the Second World War there was more employment, people became valuable. The threat of the sack became less effective because many people could easily find another job. Positive motivation became more important.

As a manager you will need to be able to motivate your staff. A manager is judged by results – and results are normally achieved through people. Motivated people achieve better results more quickly. So motivation of staff is in the manager's own interests. A successful manager motivates staff.

Take a minute to think of the most successful manager that you know. Does he or she motivate their staff?

I would be most surprised if they didn't. But *how* do they motivate their staff? There are secrets of successful motivation. All successful managers use them in one form or another. By the time you have finished this book you will have learnt to use them too.

SOME DEFINITIONS

Before we start, it might be sensible to try to define the terms that we are using.

A successful manager

Take a minute to think of your definition.

An obvious one is: 'A manager who produces the required results on time, and within budget.' I do not think that this goes far enough.

It is often said that people are an organisation's most important asset. If this is so (and I certainly think that it is) then a successful manager must make the best use of this asset. We should add a 'people' element into the definition. My revised definition would be: 'A successful manager uses people to produce the required results on time, and within budget.'

To motivate
I don't know what your definitions of 'to motivate' would be. Some I thought of were:

- ❏ To encourage, influence, inspire and stimulate staff.
- ❏ To provide them with a reason for working well.
- ❏ To make them feel that they want to work.
- ❏ To make them feel good about the work that they are doing.

If we look at the opposite, 'demotivate', we would say that someone was demotivated if they could see no reason for doing something any longer. They would feel discouraged. So – I would like to revise my definition of a successful manager again to read: 'A successful manager *motivates* people to produce the required results on time, and within budget.'

People

I deliberately used the word 'people' rather than 'staff'. This is because I think that to be successful, managers have to motivate people other than their own staff. Here is an example.

CASE STUDY

Fred is the owner of a small fishing tackle shop. His assistants Maureen and Toby are both keen fishers and enjoy their work. Fred motivates them well and they achieve high sales. They are encouraged to be very helpful to customers and spend time explaining any special techniques for using the fishing tackle. In particular they congratulate customers who have caught fish. Beginners are encouraged to come in for help and photographs of beginners with their first fish go up on a special notice board.

Fred keeps in close contact with a farmer who has a large trout lake and sells day tickets for fishing on it. He always recommends the lake to visiting fishers and the farmer, in return always recommends Fred as the best source of tackle.

Fred has motivated his staff. He has also motivated his customers and the farmer. His customers are motivated by help and praise to keep returning to the shop. Fred motivates the farmer by providing him with customers. The farmer recommends Fred's shop in return.

Fred would not be so successful if he had not managed to motivate people other than his own staff. You will learn many secrets of motivation that can be applied to other people's staff, your customers – and even your family!

MORALE

Many people think that morale and motivation are the same. They're not. A team with high morale will always be well motivated to produce results. The opposite is not always true.

CASE STUDY

In the Gulf War many of the Iraqi infantry had very low morale. They were poorly equipped and low on food and water. They were, however, very highly motivated to save their lives and get home by surrendering.

Motivation is a more basic drive than morale. Where there is high morale, staff will be motivated to produce results.

CASE STUDY

I once went to a milk-processing plant in Scotland. The plant manager had high people skills and the plant was doing well, producing excellent results. In addition there was high local unemployment and staff were reckoned to be extremely lucky to have a secure job. It was a happy plant and morale was high. The fact that the staff were highly motivated had been shown a few months beforehand. There had been a serious fire at the plant in the early hours of the morning. Word spread quickly and by four in the morning every single member of staff had turned up at the factory to see if they could help.

The manager proudly told me that this was because the staff 'were all local people, honest country folk who still valued work'.

I had seen other factories in the same area where the staff would not have voluntarily turned up at 4.00 am! I thought that he had created, through his managers, a highly motivated work force with high morale.

As managers we will want to produce the kind of motivation that is combined with high morale. That is what this book is about.

SUCCESSFUL MOTIVATORS

There is no particular type of motivator. Great motivators can have quite different personalities. Consider two great motivators: Field Marshall Montgomery and Gandhi.

Field Marshall Montgomery was a great military leader. He visited his troops in the midst of battle, talked to them individually and inspired them to risk their lives in battle.

Mahatma Gandhi led the peaceful movement against the British for Independence in India. He was self-effacing, quiet and non-violent. He inspired his followers to risk everything in his non-violent protests.

As individuals Montgomery and Gandhi were very different – yet they had both learned the secrets of successful motivation. You do not have to have a special personality to be a good motivator. You do have to have special skills. You will learn them as you go through this book.

SUMMARY

❑   A manager is judged by results, and results are normally achieved through people.
❑   A successful manager *motivates* people to produce the required results on time, and within budget.
❑   You can apply many secrets of motivation to other people's staff and your customers.
❑   As managers we want to produce the kind of motivation that is combined with high morale.
❑   You do not have to have a special personality to be a good motivator. You do have to have special skills.

QUESTIONS

1. Can you give a definition of 'a successful manager'?
2. Why should you want to motivate people?
3. Do you just have to motivate your own staff?
4. Have *you* the ability to motivate?

ANSWERS

1. A successful manager *motivates* people to produce the required results on time, and within budget.

2. A manager is judged by results, and results are normally achieved through people. Motivated people achieve better results more quickly. So motivation of staff is in the manager's own interests.

3. Many secrets of motivation can be applied to other people's staff and your customers.

4. Yes! You just have to learn the skills required from this book.

2

WHAT DOES MOTIVATION MEAN?

In the previous chapter we defined 'to motivate' as meaning:

❑ To encourage, influence, inspire and stimulate people, providing them with a reason for working well.

❑ To make people feel that they want to work, making them feel good about the work that they are doing.

These are fairly simple definitions. To look more closely at motivation we will need to consider some work done in the past by those who researched motivation in depth – the leading management gurus. Most of this work was done between 1930 and 1960 and yet senior management in many large organisations seem completely unaware of it!

In simple terms, motivation is the force that drives people to do things. Once the task has been done, the motivation may disappear.

CASE STUDY

Jane *needed* money to buy a bicycle. She wanted the bicycle very much, and was motivated to get up at 6.00 am every morning to do a paper round. After a year she had saved enough money to buy the bicycle, gave up the paper round and slept in late most mornings!

Once the *need* for money for a bicycle had been satisfied, Jane lost the motivation to do a paper round. In management the essential for good motivation is to make it last. Motivation needs to last through the time at work.

WE ALL HAVE NEEDS

The concept of *need* that motivates people has been the foundation of most motivation theory.[2]

In modern society most *basic* needs have been met – food, clothing, somewhere to live.

There are *middle-level* needs – job security, a reasonable wage, reasonable working conditions. People will not stay with an organisation unless these are being met. *Higher-level* needs will motivate people in a lasting way. These are the need to belong to a group, social status, the need to be in control of one's life, the need for self-fulfilment and pride, the need for personal development. Here are some examples:

CASE STUDY

In a wholesaler there was a survey by consultants to see if the telesales staff for orders could be replaced by an answering machine. The telesales staff knew about the survey and were worried about losing their jobs. The board rejected the proposal for an answering machine but did not tell the telesales staff this (they didn't think the staff knew about the survey). As time went by the telesales staff, having heard nothing, feared the worst and assumed their jobs would go. They became very demotivated, their work suffered and several left.

Because the need for feeling secure had not been met, the staff were not motivated. A statement from the management that their jobs were safe would have motivated them to work well by making them feel secure in their jobs.

CASE STUDY

Roger worked as a mechanic in a large garage servicing and repairing cars. He found the work very boring and stressful as each job had to be completed within a set time – even if there were complications. He was on the point of leaving to join his brother on a building site when the garage management brought in a new customer-service scheme.

Under the new scheme, when customers came to collect their cars the mechanic came out to meet them with a service checklist. The mechanic explained any problems and handed over the car. Many customers discussed their car at length with Roger, and several complimented him on his ability to sort out problems.

Roger loves his job. He feels that he is now 'somebody'. The customers value him and he feels proud of his ability to solve problems.

In the original system for repairs Roger had no self-fulfilment and pride. Under the new system he has great pride in his abilities – reinforced by the customers' praise. The new system was put in for the benefit of the customers, not the mechanics, but it had the unexpected side effect of considerably improving staff motivation.

CASE STUDY

A friend of mine, Norman, was sitting in a shopping mall waiting for his wife. He watched an elderly man sweeping away all the rubbish, with great skill. Norman said: 'That's a grand job you are doing.' At first the sweeper was upset, thinking that Norman was joking. When he realised he was serious the sweeper came over. 'Do you know, you are the first person ever to compliment me in many years of doing this job', he said. He then showed Norman some special techniques he used for sweeping and invited him to try for himself! The sweeper went back to work with a smile on his face and renewed vigour.

A few simple words of praise had given the sweeper pride and motivated him. Norman is now an expert sweeper and much valued by his wife! Motivation in this way – through the satisfying of the higher needs – is very powerful. Think back. Can you remember a time recently where you were made to feel important and wanted? Perhaps an occasion when someone praised you?

What did you feel at the time? Were you encouraged to perform better?

Praise is a powerful motivator (see Chapter 3).

PAVLOVIAN THEORY

Dogs have played an important part in motivational theory. The first experiments were done by Ivan Pavlov. He fed dogs and saw that they salivated. Next he rang a bell every time he fed the dogs. He then rang the bell without giving food – and the dogs still salivated. They *expected* food when the bell rang and acted accordingly. Later experiments with rats trained the rats to push a lever to obtain food only when the bell rang. When the bell rang and the rat pushed the lever it *expected* food.

One of the main motivational theories is expectancy theory[3]. This can be illustrated:

Performance → Reward or Punishment

If a certain level of performance is always rewarded in a certain way then the employee *will* be motivated to put in the effort to produce the required performance.

Going back to dogs, one of the first things that a puppy has to learn is to come back to its owner when called. In training for this, the puppy is rewarded with praise (and perhaps a biscuit) each time it comes back when called. It soon learns to *expect* praise for this behaviour.

Returning to its owner when called → Praise and sometimes a biscuit

In the same way, if the puppy is found chewing the owner's slipper, the owner is angry and scolds the puppy. The puppy quickly learns to *expect* a scolding.

Chewing owner's slipper ➔ Scolding

The same situation applies to young children. We give them praise when they do something that we want them to do. We express displeasure when they do something that we do not want them to do. Children want love and quickly learn to expect it when they do the thing that the parents want.

Motivation in management is not a lot different. A suitable reward – praise, a bonus, approval of colleagues – after the required performance will soon lead to expectations that a suitable performance will bring its own rewards. In the same way an unsuitable performance can lead to expectations of disapproval, loss of a bonus etc.

Are your staff receiving praise for suitable performance?

SATISFACTION

It seems that some people are never satisfied!

In the 1930s Elton Mayo in Chicago studied the results of experiments with teams of six women in the Western Electric factory. He made a startling discovery.[4]

CASE STUDY

In the original experiment better lighting was provided for one group and kept the same in a control group: output rose dramatically in both groups. Later the experimenters brought in shorter working hours, better rest breaks, incentives. Output soared. They then reverted the groups to the original 48-hour week with no special breaks or incentives. Output soared again to its highest levels!

Mayo concluded that the increases in production had nothing to do with lighting, working hours, rest breaks or incentives. They were solely due to the time the experimenters spent with each group of women explaining the experiments. The women had gained enormous work satisfaction, feeling that they were in an important team – rather than just anonymous workers in a giant company with 20,000 employees.

Most people like working in groups and being part of a team. 'Team spirit' is as important in business as it is in sport. Team spirit creates a personal pride. These experiments by Mayo laid the foundation for work by Frederick Herzberg.[5]

CASE STUDY

Herzberg questioned in detail 200 Pittsburg engineers and accountants about their feelings at work. He concluded that they were motivated by interesting work, achievement, recognition, responsibility, progress and personal growth. He found, surprisingly, that they were not motivated by salary, status, job security or working conditions. However, if any of these factors fell below a satisfactory level they became demotivated. In other words increasing salary above an acceptable level would not increase motivation. Lowering it below the acceptable level would lead to demotivation.

Think back to the example of the telesales staff in the wholesalers. They became demotivated when job security decreased. The teams of women at Western Electric were not demotivated when working conditions were reduced from a high level to what they considered an acceptable level. On the contrary – they became more motivated because they had recognition as a team.

One study of what workers want from their job[6] showed that the most important factor was steady work and steady wages (61 per cent) as opposed to high wages (28 per cent). This shows that a *middle-level* need only has to be satisfied – not exceeded.

The next most important factor was 'getting on well with colleagues at work' (36 per cent). This shows the importance of *higher-level* needs.

We can conclude from all this that most people's basic needs are met in our society.

People have to be satisfied that they have reasonable working conditions, reasonable wages and reasonable job security (their *middle-level* needs) to stay with an organisation. They will feel motivated to work harder by relating to others, having interesting work over which they have some control, having pride in themselves and what they do and being able to develop personally (their *higher* needs).

ARE WE MOTIVATED?

We have looked at what motivation is. We obviously need to identify whether or not our organisation or unit is well motivated.

Think about your organisation or unit.

Do you think it is well motivated? What are your reasons for thinking this?

You might have had a lot of reasons for your conclusion. Here are some signs that would make me think that an organisation was motivated:

❑ Employees are happy in their work.
❑ Employees cooperate rather than compete.
❑ Employees take responsibility for their work.
❑ There is a low level of absence from work.
❑ Performance is high.

Here are some signs that would make me think that an organisation had problems with motivation:

❑ Employees appearing unhappy and complaining about unimportant matters.

❏ Employees refusing to cooperate and being obstructive.
❏ Employees blaming others for their mistakes.
❏ A high level of absence from work due to illness.
❏ Poor timekeeping.
❏ Staying away from the workplace as long as possible by dragging out tea breaks, etc.
❏ Output falling below set quality and quantity standards.
❏ Jobs not being done on time.

You may have thought of different reasons for your organisation. Try ticking the appropriate boxes in the following list.

	Employees are happy		Employees are unhappy
	Employees are cooperative		Employees do not cooperate
	Employees accept responsibility for their work		Employees blame others for mistakes
	Employees rarely off work		Employees often absent
	Output always high		Output below targets
	Quality high		Quality often below target
	Tasks completed on time		Tasks often late
	Management is respected		Employees complain about management

If you have any ticks at all in the right-hand column, then you probably have motivation problems. If you have no ticks in the right-hand column you probably have no major motivational problems but can probably improve performance by improving motivation still further.

All the motivation methods that we have looked at so far have been positive methods. There are also negative methods such as fear. Fear is a powerful motivational force.

CASE STUDY

A major European electronics manufacturer had poorly motivated managers. A new chief executive was appointed to 'shake the company up' and improve performance. At the first conference of all managers, the manager in charge of the conference arrangements made a major mistake in directing the bus of delegates to the wrong restaurant. The chief executive fired him on the spot!

The chief executive hired the manager back in a private meeting the next morning but the firing had already had its effect. News of the firing spread quickly round the managers who realised that the new chief executive 'meant business' and that their jobs were on the line if they didn't perform. Performance in the company improved quickly!

I am not suggesting that you should use this method of motivation. There are other ways in which fear can be put to a

CASE STUDY

The manager of a coal mine called the workforce together. There had been a lot of disputes in the past year and production had suffered. Production was now below economic levels and the Coal Board had decided to close the pit unless it could return to profitability.

There was high unemployment in the area and the miners realised that their jobs were at risk. After a series of meetings between pit management and miners over the next three months, working practises were altered, absenteeism halved and the pit returned to profitability.

positive motivational use. These are normally in crisis situations.

This is an example of motivation from middle-level needs. The security of employment of the miners was threatened. By working harder they could make their employment secure. They were motivated to increase production.

SUMMARY

Motivation is the force that drives people to do things. People are usually motivated to satisfy needs.

Needs can be:

❏ low level – food, clothing, housing;
❏ middle level – a secure job, reasonable working conditions, reasonable pay;
❏ high level – the need to belong, to be in control, self-fulfilment, pride etc.

Low-level needs are normally met in our society.

Middle-level needs only need to be satisfied. The 'satisfiers' (eg a secure job) will not provide more motivation if increased, but they will produce demotivation if reduced below the satisfactory level. If reduced below this satisfactory level, then people may leave the organisation.

Higher-level needs motivate. These are the need to be part of a group, the need to be in control, the need for personal pride and the need for self-development.

'Expectancy theory' lies behind a lot of motivation theory. This is:

Performance → Reward or Punishment

Someone will be motivated if they can see that a particular performance will always produce a reward or punishment.

QUESTIONS

1. A large manufacturer has carried out a survey of employees and found out that they are satisfied with their working conditions. To increase production levels they spend £500,000 redecorating the factory, improving the lighting and providing the employees with smart overalls designed by a top fashion designer. Are they likely to raise production?

2. Henry has asked for an afternoon off four times in the last month: for a haircut, an appointment with his doctor, a visit to the dentist and a visit by the washing machine repair man. When his boss objected Henry got very angry and shouted that he worked hard and was entitled to get afternoons off. His boss backed down and Henry had the afternoon off.

Henry has been asked by his friend to accompany her to an afternoon performance of a film. What tactics will Henry use to get the afternoon off?

3. Sue is a homeworker knitting fashion garments. She has little contact with the fashion firm (they are very successful and sell the knitwear worldwide) who simply send her instructions and yarn. This is followed by a cheque when they get the item back completed. How might the fashion firm motivate Sue?

ANSWERS

1. Production will probably not increase as the *middle-level needs* of having a satisfactory work environment have already been met. Making the environment more than satisfactory is unlikely to work.

2. Henry's *expectation* is that losing his temper and shouting produces the reward of an afternoon off. He will shout!

3. The firm might praise Sue for her good work by letter or phone. They might tell her how successful they are, and that she is part of this successful team. This would be meeting her *higher-level needs* to have praise and belong to a team.

3

How to Motivate

In the last chapter we saw that most people could be motivated by higher-level needs. These were the need to be part of a group, the need to be in control, the need for personal pride and the need for self-development and self-fulfilment. If this is so, then we can probably design jobs in a way that will fulfil these needs and provide motivation.

CASE STUDY

A group of sales representatives used to call on customers.[7] The frequency of call, the records made after the call and the selling price that could be offered, were all specified by management.

Some jobs were redesigned. Sales representatives could decide how often to visit customers, what records to keep and – within limits – what selling price to charge. Those whose jobs had been redesigned sold almost 25 per cent more than those whose jobs stayed the same.

The fact that the sales representatives were trusted to make their own decisions, and had some control over the way that they did their jobs, made them feel valued. It is also possible to achieve the same effect without changing the job if employees are given control over some other factor.

CASE STUDY

Some years ago, as a sales manager in the publishing industry, I had a team of representatives. They had to fill in a report on each customer visited. Their selling prices were fixed. Their call cycle was fixed in that they had to call on each account each month as the books were published in monthly batches.

They could also earn a bonus on sales up to a maximum of £100 a month. They felt that this bonus was unfair, and that they had no control over it. If a 'blockbuster' was published then they easily got their £100 that month. A poor selection of books published meant they earned nothing.

I altered the bonus scheme so that each representative could choose something for which they could earn £100 a month:

- ❑ Cyril hated paperwork. He loathed having to sit in the evening filling in his report sheets. He decided to earn his £100 a month for filling in all required report sheets.
- ❑ John did not like calling on 'prospects' (shops that did not buy from us yet). He decided that he would earn £10 for each prospect that he visited.

The representatives liked the new system. Sales increased a little, but absenteeism dropped sharply and they were noticeably happier.

If employees are given some control over the work that they do, then they will be motivated. One of their higher-level needs is being met (the need to be in control).

Can you think of an example of job redesign from Chapter 2?

CASE STUDY

Roger, the mechanic in the garage, had his job redesigned. He now meets customers to discuss his work on their car. This gives him pride in his job and he receives feedback from customers on the success (or failure) of what he has done.

Work done by researchers in the late 1970s[8] suggests that if jobs are redesigned to include the following elements, then motivation, quality, output, satisfaction and absenteeism will all improve.

❏ Variety of skills: this means not having to do the same thing repeatedly. Creating a job in which several skills are required.
❏ Task significance and identity: understanding the task being carried out and its importance.
❏ Freedom: the ability to have some control over the work, and be responsible for the result.
❏ Feedback: knowledge of the actual results of the work being done.

These all satisfy higher needs. Of course the employee must have these needs otherwise they cannot be satisfied. There are some people who have satisfied their higher needs outside work (through family, through being chairman of a local society etc). There are also a few who appear to have none because of their particular psychological make-up.

How many of these elements can you identify in the job redesign of Roger the mechanic – and how many were present before the redesign of his job?

I think that the two new elements in Roger's job are *task significance* (Roger now understands better the importance of the work he is doing on a car. His discussions with customers show him this) and *feedback* (his customers tell him whether or not they are happy with his work).

I think that his job probably already had *variety of skills* (he does a lot of different types of work on cars). He probably still does not have much *freedom* as tasks have to be carried out in a specified way (manufacturer's servicing requirements etc) and within a set time.

Can you think of jobs in your organisation that could be redesigned? Job design is one of the best ways to obtain lasting motivation.

There is another way of using job design to achieve motivation and that is job rotation. If a team of operatives each carry out a separate task to complete a job, then they could swap tasks.

CASE STUDY

Usually in a large pizza factory some operatives prepare pizza bases, some prepare the toppings, some put topping onto pizza bases, and some pack the finished pizzas into boxes. In addition some specially trained operatives alter the equipment to cope with handling the new size when changing from 25 cm to 30 cm pizzas or *vice versa*. Each operative always does the same job.

In one new pizza factory that I visited, the operatives worked as a team. Operatives took it in turns to do all the jobs including altering the automatic equipment. The increased motivation of this job rotation meant that altering the equipment when changing the pizza size took half the normal time. In addition, absenteeism was lower than the normal level for similar factories.

Each operative could use a *variety of skills* during the week, rather than just using the same narrow skill all the time.

Can you think of any areas in your organisation where it would be possible to combine several jobs to allow a team to use job rotation?

IT ALL DEPENDS ON YOUR POINT OF VIEW

There is a problem with changing a job to increase motivation. It is that the role in the job varies with the point of view of the person looking at it.[9]

CASE STUDY

Shirley was personal assistant to Mary, the human resource director of a cosmetic company. When Shirley started in her job, she was given a job specification which included the preparation of the monthly Staff Turnover report. Shirley was about to produce the first report when she noticed that Mary had already started to produce it on her PC. Mary seemed to enjoy doing the report, illustrating it with complex graphs in colour. Shirley decided not to take over this task – Mary seemed to like doing it.

Mary had enjoyed doing the report the first time – she had done this to help Shirley settle into her new job. When Shirley did not produce the report the next month Mary was rather annoyed. She had to do it herself at short notice and considered that Shirley was lazy. After a year of producing the report herself she brought the matter up at Shirley's first annual appraisal.

Mary gave Shirley a low grading for 'effort' stating that Shirley was so lazy that she had to do the monthly Staff Turnover report herself.

Mary and Shirley had different views of Shirley's job. Mary knew it included the report and rated Shirley lazy for not doing it. Shirley didn't realise that Mary wanted her to do the report – she thought Mary enjoyed doing it.

If any job is to remain motivating, it is essential that both the person doing the job and their superior are quite clear about what exactly is required in the job. This may sound obvious, but there are often misunderstandings. Shirley thought she was doing her job well, but instead of praise she received criticism. Shirley found this very demotivating.

If Mary had trusted Shirley, she would have realised that there was some reason for Shirley not producing the report. Trust is a very important element in motivation. It has strong links with responsibility.

You are usually only made responsible for something if you are trusted to be able to do it. Being made responsible for something and being trusted to do it satisfy the higher needs of personal pride and can lead to self-development. You can use trust and responsibility to motivate your staff – both are powerful motivators.

CASE STUDY

I once had a new assistant – I'll call him Fred to spare his blushes! Fred came to me with a very bad report from his previous boss. Fred was 'lazy, made a lot of mistakes and had to be watched all the time', according to his record. He also had a reputation for being rude and aggressive when dealing with people from other departments and external suppliers.

I gave Fred a specific area of work and told him that it was his sole responsibility. I told him that I understood that he would be bound to make some mistakes at first but I trusted him to learn from these and not repeat them. Although he was responsible for the area, he was expected to keep me informed of his decisions.

Initially Fred did not believe me and kept coming to ask me to take decisions on every matter. I would say: 'What do you propose? That sounds fine.' After six months Fred was happily taking his own decisions and I heard from colleagues that he had stopped being aggressive and rude. His work was good and he was much happier than when he first arrived.

Fred was a good worker who had been demotivated by his previous boss who never trusted anyone. Fred found it easier to ask for his boss's decision on everything rather than risk being criticised if things went wrong. This lowered his personal pride.

When he realised that he was genuinely trusted and was responsible for his own area of work, he became motivated again.

GIVING RESPONSIBILITY PAYS OFF

Can you think back to an example of a time when you were given responsibility and were trusted – perhaps at an early stage in your career? How did you feel?

Most of us felt a little nervous at the responsibility but motivated to try hard to prove that we could do the job. You will remember that I told Fred that I expected him to make mistakes, but trusted that he would learn from them. I said this because of something that had happened to me nearly 20 years earlier.

CASE STUDY

I was working in a large retail group and was about to be given my first promotion. Before being promoted I had to have an interview with the managing director. I was terrified – and even more so when his first words were: 'Good morning, Mr Allan. Have you made any major mistakes while working for us?' I had. I was developing new products and had developed one that was a real flop. I told him this. 'Good', he said. 'When you stop making mistakes like that is when we get rid of you. Goodbye.'

It took me a week to work out what he meant. He was telling me that he valued my development work and expected me to make mistakes if I was trying really hard. I never forgot those words. Since then I have always tried to allow others to make mistakes and learn. I have not always succeeded!

If we are going to trust people and give them responsibility to motivate them, then we have to realise that they are likely to make mistakes as they learn. The art is to help them reduce their mistakes and learn from them.

We can be responsible for something and be ignored, or we can be responsible for something and be told how we are performing. I know which I prefer. Even although my performance might not be perfect, I would prefer to know about it.

To be well motivated we need to be trusted, and we need feedback on our performance. Of course we can't trust everyone – at least not straight away.

CASE STUDY

I once had a small health food shop and engaged a new manageress, Judy. She seemed to know a lot about Health Foods but I asked her to come to me with all customer queries. Each time she came with a query I asked her what she thought the answer should be. Judy was nearly always right! After two days I told her that I was happy with the way she could answer queries, and she did not need to refer to me in future.

Initially I monitored her performance. As soon as I was sure that she had the ability, I let her know that I trusted her to answer queries without reference to me. If I had continued insisting that she referred to me, she would have become demotivated and might well have left. Giving her my trust motivated her and she told me after a few weeks how much she enjoyed having responsibility for the shop.

After a month I considered the way that Judy had been working. Sales were up and customers were happy. The sales staff also appeared to be happy. Stocks, however, seemed rather low. I talked to Judy. I said how much I appreciated her good work and that both staff and customers seemed to like her. I then said that stocks seemed a bit low. Judy said she was glad I had brought up the stocks. Her previous shop had kept very low stocks but she felt that I might not agree with this policy. She had been worrying about this quite a lot. Now that I had told her, she knew that I preferred high stocks.

It was good thing that I gave Judy feedback on my feelings! She would have continued worrying about stock levels and would eventually have become demotivated. The feedback that I gave her reassured her and maintained her motivation. I might have assumed that Judy would realise that she was doing well, and also realise that I liked high stock levels. I don't think she would have realised these at all. She needed feedback from me.

Can you think of an instance where feedback helped and motivated you – and one where lack of feedback demotivated you?

There are two main reasons for feedback being a powerful motivator.

In the first place feedback is an indication that the job we are doing is important – even if the feedback is negative. It increases our self-esteem and satisfies our higher-level needs.

In the second place it fulfils 'expectancy theory'. This is:

Performance → Reward or Punishment

Positive feedback is in itself a reward, or (although this may seem an extreme description) a punishment if negative. If we are regularly receiving feedback we will learn that good performance will cause a pleasant positive feedback, poor performance will produce the opposite.

Do you give your staff feedback? If not, you are missing a very powerful tool for motivation.

We will deal with the formal use of feedback in motivation when we look at appraisals in Chapter 5. This chapter deals with informal feedback.

Of course feedback must be given correctly in order to motivate.

CASE STUDY

One of my first jobs was as a junior manager in a plastics factory. The factory produced very high quality film base that was used in X-ray photographs and in air force spy planes. The product had to be perfect. An operative had to stand in front of each machine watching the film as it emerged onto a giant roll. It was a very boring job, but when something went wrong the operative had to use considerable skill to solve the problem.

Dick was one of my best operatives with an outstanding quality record. He was saving up for a new car (his wife was disabled) and was working a lot of overtime – some weeks he worked 80 hours in total. One night he went to sleep for ten minutes on his feet in front of the machine – that was, of course, the ten minutes when the machine produced faulty film.

The next day the production manager asked me into his office to 'see how discipline was imposed'. Dick was summoned in. 'I expect you know why you are here', said the manager. 'You have caused us a serious problem because of your laziness. I am stopping your bonus for the next four weeks.'

Dick was very upset. He hardly spoke at work for several weeks. He was a shop steward in the union and relationships between the union and management deteriorated rapidly.

Obviously the manager handled Dick the wrong way. How would you have handled the situation?

CASE STUDY

Almost a year later an identical situation happened with another operative, Francis. By now I was considered experienced enough to deal with the matter myself. I hadn't forgotten Dick's reaction to my boss's harsh justice. When Francis came in he was accompanied by Dick, in his role as shop steward.

I started off by telling Francis how much I had admired his work over the last few months. Then I asked him what had happened the previous day. 'I was tired and didn't notice that the machine was producing faulty film.' 'Yes,' I said, 'that cost us a lot of money. What do you think should be the result of your failure?' 'I suppose I will lose a month's production bonus', said Francis. 'You obviously have to lose bonus,' I said, 'but a month seems a bit harsh. Considering your excellent work up to now, I think a week more appropriate'.

To my surprise both Francis and Dick agreed this was fair – and left. Francis continued to work well and was promoted to foreman a few months later.

Why do you think Francis remained motivated where Dick had not? After all, they had both received negative feedback and both lost bonus.

I think it was because I had praised Francis before offering criticism. This was not because I had thought the matter out. Francis was my next-door neighbour and I was very worried about upsetting a friend. The praise I gave was simply self-preservation!

Praise is a very powerful motivator and when used correctly in feedback will enable you to reprimand without demotivating. Of course, praise must be sincere! It is very obvious when it is not. When we praise we need to identify specific areas of performance in order to reinforce the link between performance and praise.

Performance → Reward or Punishment

Some specific areas could be:

❑ Attitude (ie cooperative)
❑ Output: both quantity and quality
❑ Development of subordinates
❑ Dealing with customers (external and internal)
❑ Contribution of ideas

You can probably think of quite a few more.

SUMMARY

1. If jobs are redesigned to include the following elements, then motivation, quality, output, satisfaction and absenteeism will all improve.

❑ Variety of skills
❑ Task significance and identity
❑ Freedom
❑ Feedback

2. There is another way of using job design to achieve motivation, which is *job rotation*.

3. You can use *trust and responsibility* to motivate your staff – they are powerful motivators.

4. *Feedback* is a powerful motivator.

5. *Praise* is the most powerful form of feedback.

QUESTIONS

1. How can you design a job to provide motivation?

2. How do you use feedback in motivation?

3. Fred is highly competent at his job but appears to be demotivated and asks you what to do before carrying out each task. What might you do to improve his motivation?

ANSWERS

1. Ensure a variety of skills is required. Give the job significance and identity. Allow some freedom in the way the work is done. Provide feedback on the results of the work.

2. It is probably always best to start feedback with some praise! You then need to tell the person concerned how you feel they are performing in their job – and the results of their doing the job. In the case of Francis and the film base machine he was told that he had not performed correctly – but also that this lack of performance had cost the company a lot of money.

3. Fred may feel that he is not trusted to do the job. You should praise his ability and show that you have trust by asking him what he would do – and trusting him to do it.

4

HOW TO DEMOTIVATE

In Chapter 2 we saw that Frederick Herzberg found some factors that did not motivate if they were at or above a satisfactory level – but demotivated if they fell below a satisfactory level. These were the factors that had to be satisfied for people to stay with an organisation. If they were not at a satisfactory level, people would become demotivated and might leave the organisation.

Can you remember what these were?

They were job security, salary, status, and working conditions. These were all middle-level needs that only had to be satisfied – not exceeded. The telesales staff at the wholesalers in our example were demotivated when job security fell below an acceptable level.

CASE STUDY

During a severe downturn in trade, a small plastics moulding company in Wales tried to cut its labour costs.

The managing director made an appeal to the workforce: 'If we all take a pay cut of 25 per cent we can survive. If not we have to close.'

The workers were on good wages. A 25 per cent pay cut still just paid their essential bills – with nothing to spare. They agreed.

Six months later the firm were in competition for a large export order. The managing director said: 'We have all made sacrifices, and now it is paying off. If we cut our labour costs by just 10 per cent we can secure this order which will guarantee our survival – and your jobs – for a year.'

The workforce refused to take any further pay cuts. In the end the managing director got rid of about 10 per cent of the workforce and the rest agreed to work unpaid overtime to make up for the lost labour.

The workers were willing to have a wage cut which reduced their wages to a level which was just acceptable in terms of meeting their living expenses. They refused a further drop. Had the managing director insisted in a cut in wages he would have had a demotivated workforce. Many would have left, or there might have been a strike. As it was the workforce remained motivated and worked extra unpaid hours. They remained motivated as long as their wages remained above the minimum they considered acceptable.

It is important to understand that the middle-level needs only have to be *satisfied*. There is usually very little permanent motivation produced if they are increased above the satisfactory level. This explains why many bonus schemes become unproductive after a period of time. At the start of the scheme the employee can see necessary things that can be bought with the extra money and will work harder to achieve bonus. As time goes on the bonus no longer buys necessary things (they have already been bought) and the employee may value a lower stress level through not continually striving to achieve bonus.

The same applies to workplace conditions. Think back to the example in Chapter 2 where Elton Mayo looked at the situation in the Western Electric works. He found that production was more dependent on interest being shown in the work teams than in increased quality of working conditions.

CASE STUDY

I once visited a factory making pies. The premises were 90-years old and the staff facilities were primitive. There was high morale and a high quality of production. Shortly afterwards the company moved to a much larger custom-built factory with superb staff facilities including a gymnasium. To the surprise of the management, although quality was maintained by rigorous controls, morale was lower than at the old factory and there was a higher rate of absenteeism.

In the old factory there was a great team spirit and people worked together to overcome the shortcomings of the old equipment and premises. They had a sense of achievement as a result. The new factory was bigger and the equipment automated. The employees no longer had any control over what they did – they just stood at a conveyor belt. The increased quality of the workplace did not motivate, and the lack of control over what they did demotivated them.

In Chapters 2 and 3 we saw that higher levels of need were great motivators if fulfilled. They are also great demotivators if reduced. In the pie factory the need for freedom – to have some control over the process – had been reduced and motivation dropped.

Demotivation can come from:

1. reducing middle-level needs below the *acceptable* level;
2. reducing higher-level needs below the *existing* level.

And these two situations can arise from:

1. the workplace and organisational practices;
2. colleagues;
3. the job itself;
4. the employee's superior (this could be *you*).

We have discussed the workplace and organisational practices (eg pay) already.

We will look at colleagues in Chapter 9, under 'teams'. We have looked at jobs and their design already – so now we come to 'superiors'.

Can you think of some of the main things a manager can do to demotivate staff? You might think of some of the things that your bosses past and present have done that demotivated you.

I expect you had a long list! Some of the main ones I thought of were:

❑ Refusal to delegate.
❑ Being inconsistent.
❑ Being unable/unwilling to praise.
❑ Lack of clear direction.
❑ Not keeping staff informed.
❑ Being aggressive and/or bad tempered.

I think that I would be demotivated if I had a boss with these faults (I have actually had one who had *all* of these faults). We will look at each of these in turn, find out how they are demotivating – and how to avoid doing them ourselves.

REFUSAL TO DELEGATE

Why do you think people refuse to delegate?

I can think of four main reasons:

1. They do not trust the subordinate to do the job.
2. They consider that they are the only people that can do the job correctly.
3. They are insecure and worried about losing control and/or authority.
4. They do not understand that delegation is productive and motivating – they are untrained.

Taken together you could say that such people lack the self-confidence to delegate. If you are going to ensure that you do not demotivate your staff by not delegating, then you will have to feel confident when delegating.

Delegation should only happen when you trust the person to whom you are delegating the task.

Supervision (over a period of time) → Trust

You will start off supervising a member of staff and, assuming they perform correctly, you will reach a stage where you trust them to carry out tasks correctly. You can then delegate to them.

It is important that you think about this process before delegating. Ask yourself the following questions:

❏ Is the person capable of doing the task that I want to delegate?
❏ Will they be able to do it without constant supervision?
❏ Will they check with me if they run into problems?

If you can answer yes – then delegate! By delegating you will be providing powerful motivation. If you delegate to someone not capable of carrying out the task then you will demotivate. That person will not carry out the job correctly and will be unhappy with the result. Their needs for praise and self-fulfilment will not be met!

CASE STUDY

Fred ran a small hardware shop. Jean was a new assistant who had only been there for a couple of weeks. A customer came into the shop just as Fred was leaving to bank the takings before the bank closed. The customer wanted a special colour paint mixed. 'You do it, Jean', Fred called out as he left, 'the instructions are on the machine.'

Jean had never used the paint mixing machine before. Although she thought that she had followed the instructions, the paint came out the wrong colour. The customer was annoyed, and Fred was angry when he came back. 'That paint is of no use to anyone', he said, 'that has cost me a lot of money.'

Jean was very upset. She had thought that she was doing well at the shop. Now she seemed to have made a bad mistake – and one that had annoyed Fred. A week later she found another job.

People don't like to fail! Jean was not at fault. Fred should not have delegated a task without being sure that he trusted her to do it.

BEING INCONSISTENT

CASE STUDY

I once had a boss who was very inconsistent and changed his mind regularly on almost every matter! At one committee meeting I presented a long report that had taken me a day to produce. He ticked me off publicly, saying that my report was on the wrong subject. I passed across to him his memo asking me to produce the report. He said, 'That was Tuesday, today is Friday – I've changed my mind.'

I found that very demotivating!

People are often inconsistent because they have not thought matters through fully. They make a snap judgement and issue instructions on that basis. Later when they have considered the matter fully they reach a different decision. This appears to staff as inconsistency – really it is lack of thought. Always think matters through fully, before issuing instructions.

Other people are inconsistent because they do not have a fixed policy.

CASE STUDY

One morning Louise asked her team leader if she could leave work an hour early to pick up her son from school as the neighbour who normally did this was ill. Her leader said that he would not agree to this. Two weeks later another member of the team made the same request and was allowed to leave early. Louise was very angry and made a formal complaint to the staff manager.

People become demotivated by inconsistency when it affects *their* work or life. If they suffer from someone else's inconsistency then they become demotivated. If they are not personally affected then they may just find it funny. My boss's inconsistency was a cause of amusement to other departments not affected by it.

BEING UNWILLING TO PRAISE

I find that not being praised is the biggest demotivator! My very inconsistent boss *did* give praise – people would have found it impossible to work for him if he hadn't.

CASE STUDY

A friend of mine, Liz, was a staff trainer for a large organisation. She worked away from head office in charge of training for a region. She came back to head office for a meeting with the senior staff trainer once a month. These meetings always centred on work that had not been done – or new work that had to be done. Liz never received any praise for her work. She was upset by this as she knew that she had the best track record for training. More of her trainees got promotion than in any other region. After three years she left to set up her own training consultancy. When she handed in her resignation

---

her boss said, 'I don't understand why you are leaving. You are our best trainer by far, and would have had a good chance of promotion this year.'

I am sure that Liz would have stayed with the company if she had been praised for her hard work. She enjoyed her work but felt unrecognised. Her need for recognition and self-esteem was not being met.

Take a moment to think about your staff. How many times in the past week have you praised them?

I found this quite a difficult skill to learn when I became a manager. It was all too easy to see what people had *not* done, or had done badly. I actually had to stop and think about the things that people had done well, and which could be praised. This was particularly difficult for people who were performing badly. I learnt that praise was even more important for them.

People are much more likely to take constructive criticism for things they have done wrong if they also receive praise for the things that they have done well. I once knew a manager, Simon, who was particularly good at this.

CASE STUDY

When Simon had to criticise some work he would ask the person into his office. He would then spend some time discussing work in general and praising some recent work that had been well done. Only then would he move on to some constructive criticism. I noticed that people always came out from such sessions motivated to do better in their job. When I asked Simon about this he said, 'It takes a lot longer than direct criticism – but the results last longer too.'

Simon also finished every discussion with the words, 'well done!'. He did this even after a session of constructive criticism.

He would say 'despite all this I think you are doing well. Well done!'. The last words that he spoke were the ones most remembered.

The ideal way to give praise is in a way that reinforces the required action. This is a three-part process[10]

❏ First: describe the action that you want to praise.
❏ Second: praise.
❏ Third: give the reason for the praise.

CASE STUDY

'Sue, I noticed that today you wrote down every phone message for me in detail. I appreciate that very much, thank you. It was especially useful as one of the messages was a detailed instruction for our next courier delivery.'

There is no difficulty here in knowing *what* action was praised, and *why* it was important to the organisation. This will motivate, and ensure the action is repeated.

LACK OF CLEAR DIRECTION

There is a lot in common here with being inconsistent as far as staff are concerned. They are receiving incomplete or conflicting information – which is demotivating.

CASE STUDY

I once worked in a large company with open-plan offices. One day the chairman walked in , looked round and said to the office manager 'This place is messy and unbusiness like. I want it put right', and walked out! The office manager was not quite sure what to do. She had the office repainted, everything tidied up and hired pots of large plants from a specialist company to give the area, as she felt, 'some class'. Six months later the chairman reappeared and was furious to see the plants. 'I want an office, not a hairdressers', he said! The office manager felt very demotivated. She had done her best with no clear direction from the chairman.

I suppose the office manager could have asked the chairman exactly what it was that he wanted. The chairman was known to have a fiery temper and the office manager was afraid to ask.

Are you sure that you always give clear directions to your staff? I am not suggesting that you have to instruct your staff in every single little detail – that would be lack of delegation. Are your staff certain that they know exactly what you want done – and are they right? Can you think of any instances where your staff did not appear to do exactly what you wanted? If so, this could be a symptom of lack of clear direction.

NOT KEEPING STAFF INFORMED

Most organisations nowadays realise, at least in theory, the value of communication. Larger organisations often have regular newsletters. These are often only papering over the cracks in their communications systems. Often the managers themselves are poor at communicating information to their staff. They think that having a formal communications system is a substitute.

Do you always keep your staff fully informed about what is going on – or do they sometimes find that decisions about things that affect them have been made on their behalf? If so, they will not have had their need for self-esteem met, and may become demotivated.

CASE STUDY

I used to work in a company that was a classic example. They had a mass of formal communication systems – company magazines, regular staff briefings, etc. However, when a new computer programme was designed none of the people who were to use it were consulted beforehand. When a totally new office layout was produced, none of the staff was asked how they would like the office laid out. As a result the computer programme was not really suited to its use and the office had to be relaid out in areas after a couple of months. Quite a few of the staff felt very demotivated. They felt that they were considered to be so unimportant that no one bothered to ask their opinion. If you had asked the company about their communications they would have told you that they probably had the best internal communications of any British company.

BEING AGGRESSIVE AND BAD-TEMPERED

CASE STUDY

I once worked for Derek, a director in a large Television and Communications company. He was always under enormous pressure and would frequently get very angry, shouting at his staff and threatening punishment if jobs were not completed on time. He was universally feared – many staff left after only a few months. Sometimes, when things were going well, he would be relaxed and jovial. He would invite everyone out for a drink after work, he would bring in flowers for his secretaries. If you had asked him, he would have seen himself as a jovial father-figure, always looking after his staff. Unfortunately they quickly forgot the flowers and only remembered the tempers.

Working for a bad-tempered boss can be very demotivating – even if you understand the pressures that cause the bad temper.

One of the problems of being bad-tempered is that we do not usually recognise it in ourselves. It is necessary to look at situations where we have been annoyed with staff and ask ourselves, 'Am I being annoyed because of a genuine failing in my staff, or am I being annoyed simply because of some external reason?'

If you find yourself getting annoyed for no good reason then you should take some time to consider whether you may be experiencing stress – as Derek was. Once you recognise that you are under stress, you can take action to minimise it.[11] Getting angry with your staff only lowers their self-esteem.

SUMMARY

❑ Middle-level needs only have to be *satisfied*. There is usually very little motivation produced if they are increased above the satisfactory level. However, if they fall below the satisfactory level people become demotivated. Middle-level needs are job security, salary, status, and working conditions.
❑ Demotivation can also come from reducing higher-level needs below the *existing* level.
❑ I thought that main demotivators could be:
  – Refusal to delegate
  – Being inconsistent
  – Being unable/unwilling to praise
  – Lack of clear direction
  – Not keeping staff informed
  – Being aggressive and/or bad tempered.

QUESTIONS

1. Can you think of three things that you might do without realising you were doing them – that would demotivate staff?

2. What factors did Frederick Hertzberg believe were demotivators if they fell below acceptable levels?

3. What is the biggest demotivator for you personally?

4. Do you think that you could be doing anything that is demotivating for your staff?

ANSWERS

1. You might have chosen from:

❑ Refusal to delegate
❑ Being inconsistent
❑ Being unable/unwilling to praise
❑ Lack of clear direction
❑ Not keeping staff informed
❑ Being aggressive and/or bad tempered.

2. They were job security, salary, status, and working conditions. These were all middle-level needs that only had to be satisfied – not exceeded.

3 & 4. I can't give you the answers to these questions! They are, however, very important. I suggest you spend some time thinking about them.

5

MOTIVATING PERFORMANCE

GOAL SETTING

Motivation can be greatly helped by the correct use of goal setting. The achievement of a goal satisfies higher needs by providing self-fulfilment and pride. Praise for the achievement of a goal provides reinforcement to the process.

CASE STUDY

In many slimming clubs, slimmers are set weight-loss goals and then weighed publicly in front of the other club members. If there is a weight loss it is announced: 'Hey, Tom has lost a massive three pounds!! Let's give him a cheer!' Everyone then cheers and applauds. This happens every time Tom loses weight. There is a special cheer if he makes his goal for that week. There may even be a certificate for regular goal achievement.

Tom is motivated because he is set an achievable goal and praised for reaching it. He is far more likely to lose weight in this way than by trying at home in private. Some American corporations use a similar method with their sales staff. There is a weekly meeting where everyone cheers when a sales representative makes target.

We can use this method in our own work situations to motivate higher performance.

Five golden rules for goal setting and reinforcement through praise have been defined as:[12]

1. Set goals that are achievable. Many small goals work better than one large one.
2. Be specific when you praise the achievement of a goal. State exactly what is being praised.
3. Give immediate praise when the goal is achieved – not later.
4. Usually praise from a superior is more motivating than a financial bonus.
5. Be a bit unpredictable – unexpected praise motivates more than expected praise!

If we think about the slimming club we can see that:

1. Small weekly goals of a few pounds are set rather than large weight losses.
2. The exact amount of weight loss is always stated.
3. The praise is given at the time of weighing.
4. The club leader gives the praise before the members join in.
5. The club leader will sometimes award a certificate.

You can see why these clubs work!

Experiments[13] have shown that the process of having clear goals set, and trying to reach them, is more motivating than the actual achievement. In order to set your staff clear goals you need to ensure that:

1. The goals are easily understood and identified.
2. The goals are achievable.
3. The goals are fair.
4. It is easy for both you and staff to tell when the goals have been achieved.

Can you think of situations in your workplace where you could set suitable goals for your staff? Would these goals fit the above criteria?

Remember that suitable goals plus praise on achievement equal motivation.

INCENTIVE SCHEMES

We saw in Chapter 2 that pay and incentives are middle-level needs. If they fall below an acceptable level, then people will become demotivated and may leave an organisation. If they are increased above the acceptable level they cease to become motivators after a time.

How can we then use an incentive scheme as a long-term motivator? What do you think could be the answer?

Incentive schemes are a very complex area and provide long-term employment for a large number of consultants! My personal view is that bonus schemes that simply relate performance to a cash bonus are, in the long run, doomed to failure.

CASE STUDY

My first job in industry was as a work study officer putting bonus schemes into a plastics factory. I soon found out that this was a game. The employees would try every trick in the book to ensure that I was not aware of the correct performance level for any task. On one occasion I spent three days with a stop-watch timing an operative fill a vat with liquids from a row of petrol pumps converted to add these liquids precisely to the vat for mixing. The whole time he had his foot on the tube to the pump nozzle so that the liquid came out at half speed. I came in at night and timed the correct flow rate of gallons per minute by using the pump myself (without my foot on the tube) and used this in the calculations for the bonus scheme.

This convinced me that such bonus schemes were limited in their application. They were more likely to be a focus for confrontation than a means to increased performance. Bonus or incentive schemes will only work in the long term, when linked to factors that satisfy higher-level needs.

Do you remember the bonus scheme I discussed in Chapter 3? You might like to recap by reading the example again (see page 27).

The reason that the scheme worked was that it was linked to higher-level needs. The representatives felt that they had some control over their own work. Their ability to set goals and achieve them gave them self-esteem and pride. Incentive schemes work best when linked to goals.

TRAINING: COACHING AND MENTORING

Why should training be considered as motivating?

I think that there are two main reasons:

❏ Training in itself can be motivating. Goals are set and achieved in the training process which lead to self-fulfilment and pride. In many cases people feel pride in the fact that time and money has been spent on their training. It is a reflection of their worth to the organisation.

❏ Training enables people to perform better in their jobs (at least, that is supposed to be the point of training!) When they perform better they feel pride and fulfilment.

Training therefore has a short-term effect in the period leading up to and during the training, and a long-term effect after the training. This effect does not last for ever. Training needs to be an ongoing process to maintain motivation.

Of course people must be motivated to learn through training. They must want the skills that the training will produce. They must see the skills they can acquire as meaningful and worthwhile for themselves.[14] Training is often imposed by the organisation. Learning only occurs with the willing participation of the employee.

CASE STUDY

When I was 11-years old I was made to learn the piano. I was trained for over two years with weekly lessons at school. I eventually was able to play very simple classical pieces (heavily adapted). I did not participate in these lessons. I suffered them. I liked neither teacher nor process. I could not see any point in being able to play the piano. Now, many years on, I cannot play the piano at all. I would like to. I would now be motivated to take lessons because I would be able to play the music that I sing. I would love to learn my singing by accompanying myself rather than having to find someone to play for me.

If training is going to be a successful motivator then:

❑ Employees must want to be trained.
❑ Employees must see that they benefit from training.
❑ Training should be structured to set goals, and provide satisfaction for achieving goals.
❑ The final skills acquired must be meaningful to the employee.

We are not going to discuss formal training methods in detail. There are, however, two processes linked to training that are part of the manager's normal functions that can be highly motivating. They are coaching and mentoring. Both these processes are linked to a new job, new skills or remedial action on existing skills.

Coaching is a process where the manager, or someone appointed by the manager, helps an employee acquire or develop skills whilst on the job – in much the same way as a tennis coach helps a player.

A mentor is someone appointed to help an employee in a new job (or, rarely, in a new skill). The mentor will be familiar with the job and available to give advice as required, but will not be doing any training – unlike a coach.

The choice of whether to use a coach or a mentor will usually depend on whether the employee lacks skills (coach), or has skills but is new to the job (mentor). A coach is an instructor. A mentor is a guide.

CASE STUDY

In one large university, each new lecturer is provided with a mentor. The mentor is an experienced lecturer who holds a couple of initial meetings with the new lecturer to pass on some hints on how to be effective. The mentor is then available to answer any queries and provide guidance for the first year.

Some lecturers are quite unfamiliar with the teaching methods used by the university. They have a coach appointed. The new lecturer attends a teaching session run by the coach to see how it is done. The coach then attends the first three sessions run by the new lecturer. At the end of each session the coach provides feedback, identifies problems and then suggests remedial action. At the end of this coaching period, a mentor takes over.

You can see how the roles of coach and mentor can interlink. They can also be used together.

The coach needs good interpersonal skills to motivate whilst coaching. Criticism should never be direct, but always a statement of the coach's feelings. For example, the coach should never say, 'you typed that report very badly', or even worse, 'You always make a lot of errors when typing reports.' She might say instead, 'I noticed that the report that you have just typed had quite a few errors. I feel that is not going to give a good impression of our department to others. How do you think we could set about ensuring the report is typed accurately?'

Note that the criticism is of a specific report that has just been typed – rather than a generalisation about all reports. The consequences of the problem are stated and an open question given to encourage discussion of the problem.

The manager, as coach, needs to:

❑ Recognise areas for development in employees.
❑ Recognise where new skills need to be acquired.

❑ Ensure that the employee sees the benefits of developments and acquisition of new skills.
❑ Facilitate the process of development or acquisition through coaching.
❑ Set development and skill goals and give regular feedback on progress.
❑ Regularly reassess the situation.

To do this the manager will need to:

❑ observe;
❑ listen;
❑ question;
❑ analyse.

Only then should a decision be made on the best course of action. In particular, whether the manager is the best coach or whether someone else should act as coach. In addition, a mentor should be considered where this is appropriate.

A mentor should be someone who is very familiar with the job, and must be readily available to give advice. They should act as a reference point for all queries.

If no coaching or mentoring is given then the employee may well feel demotivated. The fact that no one has bothered to provide help and training will lower their self-esteem. They will make mistakes, and this will again affect their self-esteem and pride.

Where coaching and/or mentoring is correctly provided then the employee will feel motivated. Their self-esteem and pride will be raised by the fact that someone thinks them valuable enough to devote time to their training. They will be set goals and will be motivated as they achieve them.

MOTIVATION THROUGH APPRAISAL

In most organisations there are two types of appraisal – formal and informal. Formal appraisals take place on a regular basis – usually annually. Informal appraisals can take place at any time that the manager wishes.

Normally an appraisal is a time when manager and employee assess the employee's performance, identify gaps in perform- ance, find ways of improvement and plan the way forward. The annual appraisal often includes a salary review. In some brave firms the employee also appraises the manager! This usually works very well.

A good performance appraisal leaves both parties feeling they have gained something.[15] A bad performance appraisal can demotivate completely.

CASE STUDY

I once was given a new assistant, Bertha, who performed very badly. Checking back on her previous appraisals I found that she was always given a glowing report, and no criticism had ever been made of her performance. As a result she had received no remedial training. In our discussion it emerged that she realised that she was not performing well, and was unhappy. She had little pride and self- esteem and was very demotivated.

After a long discussion we both agreed that she was unlikely to perform well in her existing job. She was temperamentally unsuited to it. She had been doing the job for 20 years! We agreed with the staff manager that she should transfer to a different area inside the company – she joined the design studio that suited her artistic temperament. After a year she was doing an excellent job as a design assistant, was happy and was self-fulfilled.

Bertha's previous managers had avoided conflict and carried out a meaningless appraisal each year, giving her a good report and an increase in salary. Far from being in her interests, this had given her 20 years in a job that didn't suit her, or give her satisfaction. At the age of 52 she found the area in which she could perform and be motivated – design. What a waste of 20 years!

If an appraisal is to motivate, then it must provide the employee with the means of satisfying higher-level needs. The employee must see that the results of the appraisal will further their own goals and help them achieve self-fulfilment. Only in this way will they be motivated and improve performance. This means that the whole emphasis of the appraisal should be primarily on the improvement of motivation rather than simply the improvement of performance.

This means that appraisals should be goal based. The achievement of goals should be enabled by assistance through training, mentoring, coaching or regular progress meetings (informal appraisals) with the manager. Praise should be given for goal achievement, which should be documented in formal appraisals. Only through this process can an appraisal be turned into a tool for motivating.

Some tips for appraisals:

❏ Always announce an appraisal in advance to allow for preparation.

❏ Agree a specific time, place, and specific topics for discussion.

❏ Ensure thorough preparation by both sides. Preparation by the employee is as important as preparation by the manager.

❏ Employees may wish to bring up items for discussion to add to the agenda. This should be encouraged.

❏ Find a suitable place for the appraisal where you will be undisturbed.

❏ In the meeting cover
  – an assessment of the employee's achievement of previous goals;
  – praise for goal achievement;
  – identification of needs for improvement through training, coaching, etc;
  – establishment of new agreed goals and methods for achieving them.

❏ Ensure that unsatisfactory performance is identified in a non-threatening way, and a solution agreed.

❏ Ensure that employees are fully involved in the discussion and have the chance to put over all the points that they wish to make.
❏ Ensure that employees can see how proposals made can benefit themselves.
❏ Summarise the conclusions of the appraisal – ideally in writing.[16]

SUMMARY

Strong motivational tools available to a manager include goal setting, incentives, training, ie coaching/mentoring, and appraisals.

These work as motivators through satisfying higher-level needs for self-fulfilment and pride. It is important to remember this before starting to use these tools.

Employees will only be motivated where they can see that the end product will be something that is to their own benefit.

QUESTIONS

1. What is the best method for helping an employee identify poor performance?

2. How can poor performance be put right?

3. Why does correcting poor performance act as a motivator?

ANSWERS

1. Probably a formal or informal appraisal. This has a structure that can help identify poor performance in a non-threatening way.

2. Poor performance should be improved through the setting of mutually agreed goals with means of achieving the goals, which will often involve coaching or training.

3. Poor performance is demotivating. It is stopping the higher needs of self-fulfilment and pride being satisfied. Good performance, coupled with praise, acts as a powerful motivator by providing self-fulfilment and pride.

6

LEADERSHIP STYLE AND MOTIVATION

A study of different types of leadership in boy's clubs[17] categorised leaders into:

- ❑ autocratic: where the leader decides;
- ❑ democratic: where decisions are reached by the group after discussion;
- ❑ *laisser-faire*: the group works on its own with minimal input from the leader.

Other studies indicated that if you take autocratic as one end of a scale, and democratic at the other, there are many positions in between that can be valid leadership styles. The style most appropriate to any situation will depend on the situation.[18]

CASE STUDY

If you are in a commando team under fire in a tricky situation you will need to react immediately to orders to avoid being killed. Autocratic leadership will be best. There will be little point in holding a discussion!

If you are a team of scientists working out the best methods for the next moon landing you will need a democratic leadership to ensure that everyone's expertise is brought into play. An autocratic leader might reach a quick decision that could be disastrous.

Most situations will fall somewhere between these two extremes, and most leadership styles are suitable for motivation, depending on the situation.

Can you think of a managerial situation where autocratic leadership would be suitable – and one where democratic leadership would be suitable?

I thought that autocratic leadership works best in a major crisis or where the manager's specialist skills are needed in a hurry.

CASE STUDY

Alf was the manager of a large supermarket. One winter's evening just before Christmas, all the electricity to the neighbourhood was cut off at 5 pm. The main supermarket lights went out, the tills stopped and there were still over a hundred customers inside the store. The supermarket group had trained Alf for such an emergency. To have gone to look for the relevant manuals could have wasted a great deal of time: a staff meeting was out of the question!

Alf despatched one assistant manager to start the emergency generator (which would take at least 20 mins.), got staff to take all the stock of torches off the shelves and had them standing in each aisle to help customers. He switched the tills over to battery operation and stood in the middle of the supermarket explaining the situation to customers. Within 20 minutes the emergency generator put everything back to normal. Meanwhile customers had been able to continue shopping and pay for their purchases.

A few months later I visited the supermarket. Several of the staff told me how proud they were of Alf and how they respected his taking firm control in a crisis. 'We know we can always rely on him', one said. Firm autocratic leadership in an appropriate situation had helped to motivate Alf's staff.

I expect you could think of many situations where a democratic leadership style would be suitable. I feel that this style is best suited where there is no hurry to take a decision, and where the manager is not the only one with some expertise or experience.

Staff will be motivated if you use the appropriate leadership style for the situation. In most situations the style will tend towards the democratic end of the autocratic–democratic continuum. Remember that in every organisation there will be times when an autocratic leadership is required – and a few jobs where it is regularly required.

CASE STUDY

Alf, the supermarket manager, had regular weekly meetings with his assistant managers. At these he took great care to ensure that each member of the meeting fully contributed their views. Occasionally he was deliberately 'unable to attend' and asked one of the assistant managers to take the meeting and let him know what had been decided. In this way he made it clear that he valued the views of the assistant managers and trusted them to take sensible decisions. Alf had a highly motivated team of assistant managers.

Review your own leadership style. Does it change according to the situation? You should always take time to consider the leadership style best suited to the situation that you face. This will ensure maximum motivation from your staff who will want to be led when there is an emergency, and consulted when there is not.

PROBLEMS WITH LEADERSHIP STYLES

The main problem with leadership styles in terms of motivation is when you use the wrong leadership style for a particular situation. I mentioned earlier on that there were leadership styles between the extremes of autocratic and democratic. The main 'in between' style is consultative. A consultative leadership style means that the leader consults his staff and then decides.

The three main leadership styles are:

❏ autocratic: where the leader makes the decision without consulting;
❏ consultative: where the leader consults staff, and then makes the decision;
❏ democratic: where the leader and staff form a group and make a joint decision.

Staff will feel motivated if the appropriate leadership style is used in a particular situation, and will be demotivated if an inappropriate leadership style is used.

Consider the following scenarios. What do you think is the appropriate leadership style for each, to maintain motivation?

1. *The staff Christmas party is always held after work. A decision is to be taken about what evening to hold the party – and where it should be held (within a budget limit laid down by the organisation).*
2. *The automatic mail-franking machine breaks down an hour before the last post.*
3. *The sales director has to propose budgets for the next year to the managing director.*
4. *The office committee, chaired by the administration director, has to decide what periodicals to order for circulation inside a research company.*

---

1. I thought this was a clear case for democratic leadership. The manager should allow the group of staff to make the decision about where and when the party should be held. The manager, as a member of the group, can voice her own thoughts. She may want to point out that having the party on a Friday will allow people to sleep in the next morning! The group will resent her making the decision herself. If she does take the decision then the staff may become demotivated.

2. With only an hour to go there is no time for discussion. The post room manager should appoint someone to run to the post office for some stamps! There would then still be a chance of getting the mail off.

3. The sales director will be personally responsible for the budgets. I think it unreasonable that he should make an autocratic decision on the budget. Equally it would be unreasonable to allow his sales team to reach a decision for which he must take responsibility. He should consult his team, allow discussion, but then take his decision based on consultation.

4. This is more difficult! I'm sure it shouldn't be an autocratic decision by the director. It could be a democratic decision by the committee if enough people were on it with specialist knowledge. It might be best to be consultative – the committee could circulate relevant people inside the company to suggest periodicals – and then decide.

It is not always the biggest decision that can cause the largest problem! The largest problem in the above scenarios would be caused by the Christmas Party. The imposition of a time and place could cause resentment and demotivation for a long time.

Why do you think that this could be the case?

I think the staff would feel that they were entitled to take decisions on their own Christmas party. To be denied this would mean that their self-esteem would suffer. They might feel that the management doesn't think much of them if they can't be trusted to choose where and when to hold their own party. They would also feel that they were not in control of their work life. Both these higher-level needs would be denied.

The autocratic decision-making that motivated staff in the example of the failure of power in a supermarket would demotivate staff in the example of the Christmas party.

In any decision-making situation you need to consider:

❏ The timescale of the decision – is it immediate or is there time for discussion?
❏ Who will be responsible for the results of the decision?
❏ Will staff expect to be part of the decision-making process, or only expect to be asked for opinions?

Once you have considered these questions, you can decide which leadership style to use to maintain maximum motivation.

In the above section we looked at how leaders reach decisions and give orders. In Chapter 4 we looked at the demotivating effects of not delegating, or delegating without ensuring that the person could do the task. Delegating has also a lot to do with leadership style.

Autocratic leaders rarely delegate. To delegate means to authorise and entrust. To give authority to make decisions and to trust that these will be carried out correctly. Full delegation empowers the person to take decisions – within predetermined limits. The autocratic leader will not delegate decision-taking, only actions.

CASE STUDY

Sheila worked as office manager in a firm of accountants. As each task came in, she allocated it to one of her staff to complete. When the job was finished, she would spend a long time checking it for mistakes before releasing it. Shelia felt that she delegated all the jobs that she was given – she didn't carry out any of them herself. In reality the others did the work but Sheila did not trust them and carried out rigorous checks. She was not delegating. Her staff were very demotivated and did not stay long in her department. They felt that they were not allowed to use any initiative and were not trusted.

At the far extreme a democratic leader will get volunteers for a job rather than delegate it.

CASE STUDY

Mary was department manager in a large store. She was in charge of seven assistants in the hardware department. Each day she held a brief meeting before work started and listed jobs that needed doing. She then asked for volunteers. When I joined her department, I was keen and volunteered for many jobs. I soon found that I was doing most of the work! Before I came, the other assistants had volunteered for the bare minimum and Mary had ended up doing most of the work herself.

If Mary had wanted to use volunteers then she would have needed to put in place motivators that would have ensured that people volunteered. These might have included public praise for volunteers such as, 'Sue, you have done such a lot of voluntary work today. You have been a great help. I am very grateful.' This would at least have motivated Sue.

Usually, delegation is done in the consultative leadership style. A discussion will be held on the tasks that need to be done, people will state their preferences and the time that they have available. The manager will then delegate the tasks. When this is done, care should be taken to ensure that the maximum amount of freedom is given. Where possible the exact method of doing the task should be left to the person to whom you have delegated. This allows for self-respect – a powerful motivator.

CASE STUDY

Henry, another department manager for whom I worked, was an expert at this. He would delegate the remerchandising of an area saying, 'I don't think the sales in that area are up to scratch, perhaps you could see if you could change things to produce better sales.' After the changes had been made he always gave praise. Other managers would have given explicit instructions on what needed to be done, removing any initiative from the staff concerned. Henry's staff were well motivated, and more were promoted than from other departments. They had learned to think things out and act on their own initiative. This gave them self-satisfaction and pride.

Leadership style is important in motivation, in both the way decisions are taken and tasks delegated. If both are suitable for the situation then staff will be motivated correctly.

Before you take decisions or delegate work, you must consider the task in hand and decide the best leadership style for motivation.[19] Most people will probably find that they use the consultative style most frequently – but there are always times where autocratic or democratic styles will be best. Where team work is the standard method of working, democratic management will normally be best. This is dealt with in Chapter 9.

SUMMARY

1. The main leadership styles are:

❑ autocratic: where the leader decides;
❑ democratic: where decisions are reached by the group after discussion;
❑ consultative: where the leader consults staff and then makes a decision.

2. If you take autocratic as one end of a scale, and democratic at the other, there are many positions in between that can be valid leadership styles. The style most appropriate to any situation will depend on the situation.

3. Staff will be motivated if you choose the appropriate leadership style for the situation.

4. Delegating depends on leadership style. Autocratic leaders rarely delegate, democratic leaders usually ask for volunteers; only consultative leaders regularly delegate.

5. Most situations require consultative leadership but there will always be occasions requiring autocratic and democratic styles. Only the correct leadership style for the situation will produce full motivation.

QUESTIONS

1. What are the main leadership styles?

2. What leadership style do most situations require?

3. Why is leadership style linked to motivation?

4. What are the links between leadership style and delegation?

ANSWERS

1. The main leadership styles are autocratic, democratic and consultative. *Laisser-faire* is, strictly speaking, not a leadership style as it does not involve leading.

2. Most normal management situations require consultative leadership. The main exception is where team work is the normal method. Here democratic leadership is best.

3. People will feel motivated when the leadership style fits the situation. They will be demotivated where it does not. For example, where staff face a situation where they feel that democratic leadership should be exercised – and you use autocratic leadership – they will feel demotivated.

4. Autocratic leaders rarely delegate. Democratic leaders usually ask for volunteers. Consultative leaders delegate.

7

WE'RE ALL DIFFERENT

So far we have talked about motivation as though everyone was motivated in the same way – although they certainly are not! In this chapter we will look at individual motivations, and how we can identify and use them.

Some sophisticated reward systems use multiple methods for motivation.[20] An example might be:

1. A good basic wage – to satisfy middle needs.
2. A bonus scheme for extra work produced with the names of those earning bonus posted on the notice boards with congratulations – to satisfy higher needs.
3. A 'lucky draw' for top bonus earners with a prize of a week's holiday – this acts as reinforcement for the bonus and stops bonus payments becoming part of the 'norm'.

Such complex schemes are usually drawn up by consultants specialising in organisational psychology. There are, luckily, some basic principles that we can use when considering how individuals react to motivation.

People come to work for a variety of reasons. How many can you think of?

Some that I thought of were:

❏ Most people need money, and work to earn some.
❏ Most people enjoy the company of others and relating to others. This 'social' side to work is very important for some people.

❑ Some people get bored if they are not being intellectually challenged. Work can provide an ideal challenge.

❑ Some people enjoy a particular form of work and do it because they enjoy it.

❑ Some people use work to compensate for other areas of their life. They may be unhappy and dominated at home. At work they may be able to exercise power. They may also want to be independent.

❑ Some people need a framework for their lives – work can provide this.

❑ Some people need praise and need to have self-esteem. They need personal development. They find this at work.

I suppose you could condense this down to three areas:[21]

❑ people-related;
❑ task-related;
❑ self-awareness/self-development.

This simple classification applies equally to employees, managers and leaders. In the case of leadership, people who come to work with 'people reasons' in the forefront are likely to favour a democratic style; people who come to work with 'task reasons' in the forefront may be autocratic.

Most people will come to work for a mixture of these areas, with one area more important than the others in many cases. If we are able to identify the reasons for coming to work, then we will also be able to identify the best methods for motivation.

As we have seen, basic wages only have to be at an acceptable level. Above this level they will not produce extra motivation for any length of time. Below the acceptable level they are likely to result in people leaving the organisation. In this chapter we will be looking at the reasons for people coming to work, other than for basic wages. It will be taken for granted that people are being paid an acceptable minimum wage.

PEOPLE-RELATED AREAS

These are primarily social areas:

❑ The desire to mix with, and be part of, a group of people.
❑ The desire to exercise leadership and control.

You can recognise people for whom this is an important part of work by their social interaction with others. They like talking and mixing. They do not just want to work without any contact with others. Some of them will like being in charge and giving instructions, or being consulted for advice.

Here are some examples:

CASE STUDY

Freda works on a small production line in an egg packing factory. She arrives early and spends ten minutes chatting with others in the changing room before putting on her overalls and going through to the production area. She is often seen laughing and chatting while she is working on the line and is always at the noisiest table at meal breaks. She works from 9.30 am to 3.00 pm as she has three children at school.

Freda is glad to have her children at school. Although she enjoyed looking after them when they were young and at home, she welcomes the chance to go out and meet people. The money she earns is important, without it the family would not be able to have such exotic holidays. She equally values meeting her friends at work – most of them come from the same nearby housing estate as she does. Freda's mother looks after the children during school holidays.

Although money is important to her, Freda is obviously highly motivated by her social life at work. What sort of changes at work do you think might demotivate her?

CASE STUDY

A new manager was appointed to the packing plant. He noticed that there was a large amount of gossip between the operatives on the line and felt that this was affecting work levels. He installed a loudspeaker system and paid the licence fee to broadcast the local radio station. Volume was deliberately loud so that conversation was impossible. Production levels rose, but after a few weeks Freda and several of her friends left. The company had difficulty in finding new production workers.

The manager was right in thinking that talking was lowering production levels. He did not realise that by stopping the employees from talking he was removing one of the reasons for them coming to work. Unable to chat, quite a few of them left and found other jobs. News of the 'bad working conditions' spread round the estate and made recruitment difficult.

How might the situation have been handled to increase rather than decrease motivation?

CASE STUDY

In another egg packing plant that I visited the situation was very different. There were production targets on a notice board in the canteen with achievement figures alongside. A group of operatives (all volunteers) met for a meeting once a week, paid for by overtime, to discuss methods of achieving targets. The manager was not present, but they reported their findings to him. Each month there was also a social outing – bingo, tenpin bowling, etc. There was a monthly newsletter giving details about employees and their families.

The employees enjoyed the monthly target meetings and came up with quite a few good ideas for increasing production. They still

---

> chatted on the line, but not at the expense of production. The social outings and newsletter made them feel part of a large 'family' and they enjoyed coming to work.

The manager at this factory understood the social needs of his employees. He built on them and utilised them through the voluntary target meetings. The social outings were open to families and this brought operatives' partners and children into the social scene. Very few people left for other jobs and the factory had one of the highest productivity ratings in the group.

Think about your own workplace. Can you identify people who come to work for social reasons as well as for money?

I would be surprised if you could not think of any! If you wish to motivate such people then you must ensure that:

❑ You do not demotivate them by removing the ability to enjoy social interaction.
❑ You find ways of motivating them by using their desire for social contact (without, of course, decreasing work levels)

Some common ways of motivating socially include:

❑ The use of notice boards for personal messages and advertisements.
❑ Provision of a news sheet, however basic or small, giving personal information and news.
❑ The encouragement of joint social outings.
❑ Formation of employee groups to come up with ideas.
❑ An attitude from the manager that encourages chat that does not interfere with work.
❑ Provision of targets and achievement figures that can be discussed by employees.

There are, of course, many more. You might like to think of the ones most suited to your workplace.

CASE STUDY

Rudi was 62, had come to Britain from Poland after the Second World War and had recently joined the provincial office of an insurance company from Head Office, as he intended to retire in the area. He was very keen to mix with others at first, but the rest of the office staff were under 30. He was left out of most conversations and spent meal breaks on his own. His work slowly deteriorated and became unsatisfactory.

The office manager, Helen, noticed this and gave a lot of thought to the problem. She decided on two courses of action.

1. Rudi had great experience of head office procedures, which were not fully understood by those in the provincial office. Helen appointed him 'Head Office procedures guru' and asked anyone with procedural problems to consult Rudi.
2. In chatting to Rudi, Helen found that he wrote poetry and arranged for one of his poems *A Child's Christmas in Poland* to be published in the area newsletter.

Over the next few weeks Rudi changed completely. He took great delight in explaining procedures – he enjoyed passing on his knowledge – and in the respect he gained from the rest of the staff who had never realised how much he knew. His poem about the death of his younger sister from starvation in Warsaw on Christmas Day 1945 brought tears to many eyes. He was asked for more details of the situation in Poland at that time, over lunch the next day.

Rudi's work output improved greatly. He also became friendly with the parents of several staff members who were introduced to him at the annual Christmas party. He no longer felt left out in the office social scene. The time that Helen had spent trying to work out how to integrate Rudi into the social scene had paid off!

If you have an individual who is not 'fitting in' to the workplace, then time spent on thinking about how to motivate them is well spent. How you any similar people in your workplace? How would you motivate them?

TASK-RELATED AREAS

These are areas where the job being done is more important than the social side of work. This is not to say, of course, that there is no social side. The job itself is simply more important.

CASE STUDY

In a large hospital trust there was a small haematology laboratory with four technicians. The demand for their blood tests was high and they were regularly working overtime. Although all four were dedicated to their work and took great pride in the accuracy of their testing, the manager noticed that there was a higher absenteeism than in other areas of the hospital. After checking the absence records of the technicians she decided that the problem was a motivational, not a medical, one. She talked at length to the four and found that they felt isolated. Their tests had become a meaningless routine.

The manager arranged for each of the technicians to spend a day with the consultant haematologist and the operating theatre sister. Their task was to find out the reasons for carrying out the tests in the laboratory, and to determine any improvements that could be made.

The tests were found, on the whole, to be adequate in their present form. Despite this, absenteeism dropped and the technicians seemed much happier. They had seen for themselves the usefulness of their tests, and their place in saving lives in the operating theatres. They felt part of a larger team and could see the part that their skilled work played in the team effort. The tasks that they performed in the laboratory took on new significance and importance.

You can recognise people for whom this is an important part of their work by the importance that they attach to the task in hand. They will tend to put work first, to find it very important that work is done correctly, and to have particular work skills.

Where people come to work primarily for task-related areas, they will best be motivated if they can see the importance of their task and its relevance to the output of the organisation.

Do you have people in your workplace who are task oriented? Do you think that they can see the importance of their task – and where it fits in? If not, they are likely to become demotivated.

SELF-AWARENESS/DEVELOPMENT AREAS

These areas are very powerful for motivation and represent the higher levels of motivation.

It is not always easy to recognise people for whom this is an important part of their work. If they are not already finding self-fulfilment in their work, they may not be aware of this higher-level need. They may simply be dissatisfied with their work without realising why. For this reason it is safest to assume that all employees have a need for self-awareness and self-development (leading to self-fulfilment).

Self-fulfilment can be expressed as pure self-interest.

EXERCISE

I know an author who writes his books for his own pleasure. He enjoys the research and the writing and would not be really worried if the books were not published. His reason for book writing is pure self-fulfilment. He enjoys the intellectual exercise. He is not primarily task focused, his books are not particularly well written. His focus is primarily on the research. His books are on a narrow subject area that interests him greatly.

Other people will reach the higher level of self-fulfilment as their main reason for coming to work through either task or people focus. They may work for several years with task or people as their main reason for work but will eventually find the need for self-fulfilment greater.

People who come to work for self-fulfilment are likely to respond well to praise, to be interested in learning and to be interested in improving their performance.

CASE STUDY

Ruth came to me after finishing her year as a graduate trainee. Her last three months had been spent in a boring clerical job which consisted of entering a large amount of data into a computer. She did not appear to be particularly interested in her new job and was often late for work.

Ruth's trainer told me that Ruth had been highly motivated when she first joined the company, but that her last job had been very demotivating. Ruth had been overheard telling another trainee that she was looking for a job elsewhere.

I gave Ruth an area of her own to work on with full responsibility. I also arranged for the company to sponsor her on a basic management course, which was distance learning from the Open University and took six months to complete.

Ruth found self-fulfilment in taking and passing the management course, which she found very challenging. She also got great satisfaction from performing well in her area of responsibility and enjoyed the praise for her achievements. She was not particularly interested in the task of running her area, but enjoyed the intellectual challenge of reaching her targets.

Ruth had some task interest, but her prime interest was in self-fulfilment. She remained for several years until a change in management structure, which made her less responsible for her area, was coupled with her application for funding for a further management course being turned down. She left. Her higher-level needs for self-fulfilment and self-development were no longer being met.

A PERSONAL APPROACH

To achieve maximum motivation it is necessary to tailor the motivation to the individual. In order to do this you first have to assess the individual and determine the areas – people, task and self-fulfilment – that need to be addressed. You can best do this by observation of the employee in the work situation. Some tests[22] are available to determine personality types, but personality types do not always follow motivational patterns. It has been argued that extroverts are more focused on people, introverts on task and that people motivated by self-fulfilment tend to be reflective. In my experience this is not always the case!

When considering an individual you need to ask yourself a series of questions. Ideally this should be done after an appraisal where you will be able to discuss areas that will help you make your judgement. There are several books available[23] with suitable sets of questions, and also specialist firms who can undertake testing.*

Sample questions would be:

❑ Is this person at ease with people? Do they enjoy the social life of the workplace.
❑ Do they show leadership abilities, and do they like being in control?
❑ Are they introvert or extrovert?
❑ Do they tend to focus on the task in hand to the exclusion of everything else?
❑ How do they react to praise?
❑ Are they group dependent and a joiner of groups, or are they more self-sufficient?
❑ Are they interested in 'bettering themselves'?

From asking yourself a series of questions such as these, you will be able to form a reasonably accurate estimate of whether someone is people, task or self fulfilment oriented. You will then

---

* EITS, 83 High Street, Hemel Hempstead, Herts HP1 3AH, 01442 256773, are a good example.

be able to plan how to motivate that person. Remember that many people will have a mixture of the three areas.

SUMMARY

1. People want to work for reasons connected with three main areas of needs:

❑ people-related;
❑ task-related;
❑ self-awareness/self-development.

This assumes that their basic requirement for an acceptable wage has been met.

2. By identifying one or more of these areas as the main reason for someone wanting to work, you will be able to work out the best means of providing motivation.

3. You can best identify the areas during a formal discussion such as an appraisal, or by asking yourself a series of questions about that person.

QUESTIONS

Can you identify the need areas that make these people want to work? What sort of action would you take to motivate them?

1. Henry works in a double glazing company as a specification clerk. His job is to take the details of the windows written down by the salesmen and convert them into specifications for the factory to manufacture. Head Office where he works is 50 miles from the factory – the specifications are faxed over. Henry is very meticulous and double checks every figure that he calculates. He will often work through his lunch break if he has a lot of orders to specify. He is very quiet and takes no part in the office social life. At meal breaks he sits by himself and reads a book on biology – he is taking a course in the evenings at the local college.

2. Sheila works in the accounts section of a large firm of management consultants. The accounts office is on the ground floor and has the reception desk at one end of it. Sheila is very interested in other people and at meal times she is usually to be found with another member of staff having a long discussion. You have noticed that she gets bored after a couple of hours working on her computer and then tends to wander round the office chatting and distracting others.

ANSWERS

1. I think that Henry is probably mainly task oriented – although he also has a strong element of self-development in his needs. Perhaps he could visit the factory for a day and see how his specifications are turned into windows – and even go out with a salesman to see how orders are taken. The company could encourage his interest in evening classes by giving him a day off for revision before his exam. If he was treated in this way he would be motivated by finding out how his specifications were used, and be pleased that the company were supporting him in his evening classes.

2. I think that Sheila is people oriented but in a task-work environment. I wonder if she could act as relief receptionist at meal breaks. This would enable her to meet a lot of different people and might satisfy her need for social contact. It might also stop her wandering about chatting!

You might have different views on how to motivate Henry and Sheila. You should, however, have been able to identify Henry as basically task oriented and Sheila as basically people oriented.

8

MOTIVATING DIFFICULT PEOPLE

So far we have assumed that people are happy to be motivated, but this is not always the case! In this chapter we will be looking at ways of motivating people who are 'problems' in terms of motivation.

UNACCEPTABLE BEHAVIOUR

A common problem is trying to motivate people who behave in an unacceptable way, to behave correctly.[24] As an example, someone may use bad language which offends others, and you wish to motivate them to stop using bad language. To do this we can use positive motivation or negative motivation (sometimes referred to as reinforcement and suppression).[25]

For positive motivation either something that is liked is given, or something that is disliked is taken away. For negative motivation something that is liked is taken away or something that is disliked is given. Negative motivation is often seen as 'punishment' and has been shown in research evidence to be less effective than positive motivation.[26] For this reason we will only deal with positive motivation in this section.

In order to motivate the stopping of unacceptable behaviour we first have to look at three questions:

❑ What is the unacceptable behaviour? Can we define it precisely? For example, 'Jason tends to use bad language when talking to other members of staff.' (He doesn't use it when talking to customers.)

❑ What reinforces his unacceptable behaviour and keeps it going? For example, 'Several of Jason's colleagues on the sales team laugh at his bad language and encourage it'.

❑ Can we define exactly what behaviour we do want? For example, 'We would like Jason to be as courteous to staff members as to customers.'

When we have answered these three questions, we have analysed the situation. We know what the unacceptable behaviour is, what reinforces it and what behaviour we would like. We now have to decide how we can motivate the required behaviour. In order to do this we have to ask two more questions:

❑ What things motivate Jason? We might find that Jason is motivated to come to work for self-fulfilment reasons, and likes to display his skills and knowledge to others.

❑ What things demotivate Jason? We might find that Jason is demotivated by the attitude of the accounts department towards the sales team's expenses.

Now that we have identified these two areas, we can form a motivation plan to eliminate Jason's unacceptable behaviour. To do this we must:

❑ State the unacceptable behaviour.
❑ Indicate the target acceptable behaviour.
❑ Indicate the motivators to change the behaviour.

In Jason's case we might say:

> Jason, I have noticed that a lot of the office staff are upset by your bad language – I also find it offensive. I have also noticed that you never use it when talking to customers. We are looking for a sales team member to give a talk to the accounts team in a few months time, to help them understand the requirements of sales when it comes to expenses. With your skills and knowledge you would be ideal for the task, but your continual use of bad language makes

this impossible. If, however, you can show that you can talk to office staff over the next couple of months without using bad language, then I would be very happy for you to give the talk. I think it would be very helpful in improving the accounts department's understanding of sales problems.

This is, of course, a great oversimplification of the process. You would have to take a great deal of time considering the situation and Jason's motivations. You would also spend much more time talking the situation through with him than I have indicated above. The basic principles still apply despite this. In the example above Jason would be motivated by the chance to display his skills and would also be keen to remove the demotivating effect of the accounts department's attitude. In order to do this he is likely to be willing to change his behaviour.

After the initial motivation for change, it is necessary to reinforce the change on an ongoing basis. In the example above you might talk to Jason regularly and praise his changed behaviour. You might say:

Jason, the accounts department really enjoyed your talk, and I have been very impressed with the change in the way you talk to office staff. I wonder if we could ask you to give a talk to some of the secretaries in a few months time?

A change from unacceptable to acceptable behaviour will have to be continually reinforced.

TALENTED, BUT LACKING MOTIVATION

I have found this very common in my experience. People in this category fall into two classifications: those who are new to work (trainees: whether straight from school or graduate entry) and those who are already in work.

New to work

Employees who are new to work may have come straight to work from education, or may have had a spell of unemployment. Many of them will not be motivated because they only see work as a means of earning a basic wage. They are probably not married, do not own property and only need money for daily spending. Many may still be living at home. They are unlikely to be interested in large amounts of overtime, or in working very hard for a bonus payment. They may not see any advantage in promotion, it only brings extra responsibility and 'hassle'! They may also not be particularly interested in training – which they see as an extension of school.

With new employees like this, you will probably not know what is likely to motivate them and they will not have had enough experience of work to know what they like. This means that you will not have identified whether they come to work for people, task or self-fulfilment reasons. They may only come to work to obtain spending money! You assume that they have talents, hidden at this stage, and wish to motivate them.

The two 'needs' that such people are likely to have are the middle-level need of belonging to a group and the upper-level need for praise. These are not very different from the needs they had in education.

The need to belong to a group will be met by the immediate colleagues that they work with and the social facilities provided for the organisation as a whole. In a small working group new employees need to be integrated into the group and feel part of it. This can be partly achieved through a good induction process, and partly by care being taken to make employees feel 'at home' through simple things like asking about their hobbies and leisure activities. In a larger organisation social activities need to be provided for this age group – not just for the older employees.

The need for praise means that these new employees should either be on a properly organised training scheme, or else be provided with a coach or mentor (see Chapter 5). The coach may be you, their manager, in which case you must ensure that you motivate correctly through praise.

CASE STUDY

Tracy joined the accounts department of a District Council straight from school. She had passed her English and mathematics exams – but nothing else. She seemed to have no interest in work and was just waiting for the end of each working day when she could go home to get ready for a 'night out'.

Helen, the accounts manager, felt that Tracy had hidden talents. Tracy had been given a two-day induction into the Council and the accounts department but, as she was employed as a filing clerk, there was no formal training scheme. Helen decided to tailor a motivation package specifically for Tracy. She decided on the following:

❑ Each day at coffee break she made sure that she asked Tracy how she had got on the evening before.(She first of all checked that Tracy liked talking about her evenings!) She showed interest in Tracy's activities.

❑ She appointed Sue, who had joined from school four years ago, as Tracy's mentor. Sue had started as a filing clerk but was now a section leader. Sue was to talk to Tracy at least once a day to check how she was getting on.

❑ The section in which Tracy worked had the Housing Department accounts as a major workload. Helen arranged for Tracy to spend an afternoon with one of the Housing officers to see how the Housing Department worked, and why bills came in for payment.

❑ She praised Tracy whenever a particularly large batch of filing had been done, and did this so that the rest of the staff could hear.

❑ The Council had a social committee and Helen encouraged Tracy to suggest that visits to the local disco should be part of the social activities. Tracy was asked to help organise the first of these events.

Nothing that Helen had done was particularly special – she just made sure that Tracy was integrated into the work group and received praise and attention. Within three months Tracy obviously enjoyed coming to work, was doing a good job, and had asked to be considered for training as an accounts clerk.

Not new to work

Employees who appear to have talents but lack motivation, and who have been employed for some time, are likely to have been demotivated in the past. Alternatively they may never have been motivated when they first started to work. In either case you should determine whether they come to work for people, task, or self-fulfilment reasons (see Chapter 7) and tailor a motivational package accordingly.

UNWILLING TO TAKE RESPONSIBILITY

These employees are either unwilling to take responsibility for their own work, or are unwilling to take responsibility for the work of those reporting to them.

There can be a number of reasons for this, and it is important to identify them before determining a method for motivation.

What reasons can you think of for someone being unwilling to take on responsibility?

Some that I thought of were:

❑ Insecurity. The employee may not feel 'up to' the job. They may be lacking in skills, or feel unable to cope with other employees.
❑ Lack of self-confidence. The employee may realise that they have the skills required, but lack the self-confidence to take on the responsibility.
❑ The employee may be afraid of under-performing or making mistakes.
❑ The employee may be unwilling to accept criticism, and may feel likely to be criticised if they accept responsibility.
❑ The employee may dislike, or be afraid of, some other employee with whom they have to work closely.
❑ The employee may see no reason to take on the extra hassle of the responsibility.

There might be a lot of other reasons; you probably thought of some. If you have an employee who is unwilling to take on responsibility you will first have to identify the reasons, and then plan to counteract them and provide motivation.

For example, in the first three above, you might decide to provide training or coaching to increase skills and confidence. You might also be careful to praise and encourage progress. By doing this you would be helping to eliminate the barriers to taking on responsibility, and at the same time providing motivation by meeting higher-level needs for self-esteem.

The process is:

❏ Identify the restraints to taking on responsibility.
❏ Take steps to eliminate or minimise these restraints.
❏ Provide support for the process of taking responsibility.
❏ Provide suitable motivation to encourage the taking of responsibility.

CASE STUDY

When I was a buyer I once had an assistant, Barbara, who worked part time. She had no formal responsibilities but in reality was doing a very responsible job. I wanted her to become full time and take on the responsibilities of a deputy buyer.

Barbara was very unwilling to become a deputy buyer. She felt unable to take on the formal responsibilities although she was already performing all the duties of a deputy buyer. She felt very happy doing the job, but unhappy in accepting the responsibilities of the job.

When I discussed this with Barbara I found that she did not have confidence in her abilities, which I rated very highly. She did not see herself as a 'business woman' but rather as a mother doing an interesting part-time job. I spent three months encouraging her to take responsibility for the job, bit by bit. I also told her of my respect for her abilities, which was also felt by a lot of her colleagues. After three months she became confident enough to become a full-time employee, and was promoted to deputy buyer. She became one of the best deputy buyers that I ever had.

The situation with Barbara was not complicated. If, however I had tried to push her straight away into becoming a full-time deputy buyer, she would almost certainly have refused. She might even have left. She needed to gain confidence in her abilities. She was also motivated by her success (self-fulfilment) and my praise.

There is no single formula for motivating those who are unwilling to take on responsibility. You will have to consider each case individually and work out a motivational plan.

RESENTFUL OF YOUR POSITION AS MANAGER

This could be for several reasons. How many can you think of?

I thought of:

❑ They had been passed over for promotion in the past.
❑ They had been in competition with you for the position of manager.
❑ You are young and they are much older. They do not like someone younger in charge of them.
❑ You are the opposite sex and they do not like someone of the opposite sex in charge of them.
❑ They do not want change – and you might bring it!
❑ You do not show any interest in their work.

You might have thought of a few more. People who are resentful of your position as manager are unlikely to be motivated to work well. You will have to reduce or eliminate their resentment before you can start to motivate them. As in the case with people unwilling to take responsibility you must:

❑ identify the reasons for resentment;
❑ take steps to eliminate or minimise these reasons;
❑ provide suitable motivation to restore performance.

The reasons for resentment are usually very powerful – and not easy to eliminate. You will have to accept the fact that you may not be able to eliminate them in the short term. If you are unable to eliminate the resentment, then it will be necessary to negotiate a working arrangement to minimise the resentment.

CASE STUDY

A year after I left university and joined a chemical company I was promoted to production manager of part of the factory. Most of the other managers were over 40 (this was 1963 and the Second World War had resulted in a shortage of mature managers) and the foremen reporting to me were in their 50s. I was very self-confident and felt that I knew better than anyone else. I was unskilled in observing others and did not notice the resentment at my promotion. After nine months I was taken off the job and sat in an office with a newspaper – *The Times* – open at the appointments page!! I wasn't sacked as I was performing well in my job, but the resentment of others forced the managing director to drop this heavy hint that I should leave. I left!

Because of my inexperience and arrogance I did not even consider that people might resent my position as manager. Even if I had realised this, I would not have known how to cope with it. It is not always easy to spot resentment. People may try and hide it. If you have an employee working for you who appears to be demotivated, or working below potential, then you should always consider the possibility that they are resentful of your position. Tell-tale signs might include:

❑ Talking about you behind your back.
❑ Being unnecessarily polite or deferential.
❑ Criticising your decisions.
❑ Not cooperating in matters that affect your personal business reputation.

If you feel that someone resents your position, whatever the reasons for the resentment, it is best to bring the matter into the open and discuss it.

CASE STUDY

I was once brought into a book-publishing group as sales manager. I had no experience of publishing, or of selling. I had been brought in because the whole sales operation had to be reorganised after the amalgamation of six publishing companies into the group. The group chairman had heard me give a talk at an international conference and thought I could do the job!

All the original sales staff of the six companies had been sacked, apart from one man, Norman. He had been the sales director of one company and had been kept on as a sales representative. This was a big demotion but, at 60 years old, Norman did not have any option but to accept.

Luckily I had gained some experience since leaving the chemical company. I had a private meeting with Norman. I told him that I had been brought in for my skills at reorganising and that I had no skills at selling or in publishing – but I was happy to learn. I told him that I understood that he must be very resentful of my appointment and that in his position I would be resentful too. I suggested that we could work together. I would do everything that I could to help him. I would make it clear to all his old customers that I valued him greatly, I would be willing to listen to his advice and would consult him on matters concerning selling and publishing. When the sales team was rebuilt I would make it clear that he was the most senior and most valued member of the team. In return I asked for his support in my position and in my reorganisation of the sales department.

I had a very happy relationship with Norman. He taught me a great deal and retained the respect of the buyers of the major companies that he had always dealt with. I always made it clear, when we were with these buyers, that Norman was the expert, not me. With his help I successfully reorganised the sales department – and I realised that I could not have done it without him.

This situation only worked because Norman and I had an honest discussion and both admitted the problem in my appointment after his demotion. He was motivated because I made it obvious that I valued his experience and boosted his reputation with his major customers – meeting his higher needs for self-fulfilment and self-respect.

In this chapter we have dealt with four common problem areas. You will obviously come across other 'problem people' but the approach should always be the same:

❏ identify the problem;
❏ decide on the best method to minimise or eliminate the problem;
❏ decide on the best method to motivate by identifying the 'needs' that you can meet.

SUMMARY

1. Where you need to motivate people who have unacceptable behaviour:

❏ state the unacceptable behaviour;
❏ indicate the target acceptable behaviour;
❏ indicate the motivators to change the behaviour.

2. Where you have to motivate people new to work who are talented, but lacking in motivation, the two 'needs' that you must address are the middle-level need of belonging to a group and the upper-level need for praise. These are not very different from the needs they had in education.

3. Where you wish to motivate people unwilling to take on responsibility you need to:

❏ identify the restraints to taking on responsibility;
❏ take steps to eliminate or minimise these restraints;
❏ provide support for the process of taking responsibility;
❏ provide suitable motivation to encourage the taking of responsibility.

4. If you feel that someone resents your position, whatever the reasons for the resentment, it is best to bring the matter into the open and discuss it.

5. In general when dealing with 'problem people':

❑ identify the problem;
❑ decide on the best method to minimise or eliminate the problem;
❑ decide on the best method to motivate by identifying the 'needs' that you can meet.

QUESTION

Darren has just joined your department from school. He appears to be highly intelligent (he can correct computer problems that your engineer can't!) but is not interested in working, and uses bad language. What might you do to motivate him?

ANSWER

You have two problems – unwillingness to work and bad language.

To motivate to work you will need to use the methods outlined in the section *Talented, but lacking motivation.* The two needs that you need to address are the middle-level need of belonging to a group and the upper-level need for praise.

To motivate Darren not to use bad language you will have to use the method outlined in the section *Unacceptable behaviour.*

9

MOTIVATING TEAMS

Many organisations are having to cut costs in order to remain in business. They have already cut staff numbers to the bone and are having to turn to other methods of lowering staff costs.

---

*How can organisations lower staff costs in some areas by as much as 25–30 per cent?**

My answer is that many organisations now use teams as their preferred format for working. The old line-management structure is gradually being replaced. In many organisations the position of 'team leader' is a permanent one, and team leaders go from one project to another. They build a new team for each project with team members chosen for their specific skills for that project.[27]

The result of using teams in this way is a change from line-management structure to a 'matrix' structure (where an employee reports to more than one boss).

A team member, Bill, may be responsible both to the boss of his 'skill area' (his functional boss) and his team leader. For example a computer programmer on a team will be responsible to the IT director for the overall effectiveness of his work, and to the team leader of a specific project for his performance on that

---

* A figure from research that I carried out over a year through questioning members of teams from various organisations in both the public and private sectors.

	Sales Director	IT Director	Engineering Director	Admin Director	
					Team 1
		● Bill			Team 2
					Team 3
					Team 4

project. He will also carry responsibility to the other team members for his role in the closely integrated team effort.

CASE STUDY

I met Harry when he was taking an MBA. with the Open University. He was employed by a large multinational company as a team leader. He had just finished a major installation project in India and was about to start one in the Middle East. He started work on a project two years before installation and gradually built up the team that would oversee the installation using local contractors. A member of the local contractor's company and the local architect joined the team six months before installation.

Harry told me that the team format gave him particular motivational problems. Many team members would only be on the team for around nine months. Their pay and promotion was agreed by their functional director, not Harry. They felt temporary loyalty to the team but their long-term loyalty was to their functional director. Some members of the team were not even employed by Harry's organisation. Their loyalty was to their own company – and to the project. A particular problem was the team member who was employed by the local contractor. That member got paid a bonus by the contractor according to the profit that the contractor made. The higher the profit that the contractor made, the lower the profit made by Harry's organisation!

I think that teams pose greater motivational problems than individuals in the normal line management structure. Can you think of some reasons why this might be so?

Some that I thought of were:

❏ Team members will belong to two social groups, the team and their functional group (ie their skill group – the engineering department, the training department, etc).

❏ Team members will have been trained in their functional group. Their boss and their coach (if they had one) will not be on the team.

❏ Team members' middle-level needs for job security and a reasonable wage will be provided by functional management outside the team (for example the engineer will be rewarded by the engineering director). The middle-level need for reasonable working conditions may be met partly inside and partly outside the team.

❏ Team members will receive higher-level needs mostly from the team situation, but also from their functional position outside the team (for example the training specialist will receive self-esteem from others in the training department admiring her work).

❏ In many teams, although there is an overall team leader, the person actually leading the team at any time will depend on the function that the team is carrying out. For example if the team is working on the specification for a building then an architect or surveyor may be leading the team at that point.

When the team moves on to costing the project, an accountant may take over as temporary leader. Many teams work in this way.

You probably thought of others – teams are complex structures!

TEAM MOTIVATION

A team as a whole can be motivated in the same way as individuals. Primarily motivation comes through higher needs. Usually teams are task oriented and take pride in successful completion of the task for which they were formed. Teams also have a need for self-esteem. For these reasons teams can be motivated by praise and by seeing the ways in which the task that they are performing fits into the operation of the organisation as a whole.

CASE STUDY

A large retail group set up a team to implement new computer systems in Head Office and individual stores. The team operated for a year and had complete control of the implementation. Regular progress reports on the team's work were published in the monthly company newsletter and the managing director appeared regularly at team meetings to congratulate them on their progress. The computer manufacturer told the team that they were the first to install such a system and made a presentation to explain to the team how the new system would improve the performance of the store group.

The team felt highly motivated and completed the schedule well ahead of target. A year after the project had finished team members were still saying how much they had enjoyed working on the team.

In this example the team was motivated in the same way as an individual.

A team can be considered as being motivated in three areas:[28]

Task: the group's common achievement of the task for which they were established.

In the above scenario, the team did a good job, and were regularly congratulated. This gave them self-fulfilment and a pride in their work as a team, and as individual team members. A good team leader ensures that the team is motivated by achieving in its task.

Group: the group's social needs for interaction between members.

A good team works and plays together. Team members support each other and enjoy each other's company. A good team leader ensures that the members of the group socialise and have good relations with each other. Any personal conflict and friction must be dealt with quickly.

Individual: the individual needs of different group members.

MOTIVATION OF INDIVIDUAL TEAM MEMBERS

The motivation of individuals in teams is made difficult by the problems outlined at the start of this chapter.

First ask yourself some questions about each team member:

❑ Is the team member an employee of your organisation or an outside organisation? (If an employee of an outside organisation, they may be more motivated to perform for that organisation than for your team.)

❑ Is the team member happy to be on the team? (If not, you will have to pay special attention to motivating them to be part of the team.)

❑ Is the team member a specialist with high-level skills? (If so, they may be highly task motivated and less interested in team performance.)

❑ Has the team member been in a team before? (If not, you will have to provide motivation to integrate them into the team, and provide training in being a team member.)

Since the members of a team have to work as a team, all the members have to be motivated by being on the team. If this is not the case then they are unlikely to perform properly as team members. Being motivated by being on the team means that their needs must be met by being on the team. Middle-level needs such as salary and working conditions will be met by the organisation. Higher-level needs such as belonging to a group, social status, being in control of life, self-fulfilment and pride, and personal development, will have to be met by the team.

CASE STUDY

Jenny worked as a trainer in a District Council. Her job had originally been as a trainer inside the training department providing a wide range of courses to all parts of the Council. The Housing Department had decided to implement a new structure coupled with new methods of working using the latest computer and communications technology. The aim was to cut staff costs by 30 per cent. A team had been set up to design and implement the new system. Jenny had been appointed to the team to design a training scheme to enable staff to implement the new system.

When Jenny arrived, the team had already been working on the design of the new systems for six months. Initially Jenny felt lost and quite frightened. The team worked in an office 20 miles from her training department, she had never met any of the team members and she was supposed to be the 'training expert'! She was introduced to the other team members on the first day and given a presentation on the systems which had been developed. On the second day she had a special training session on 'Team membership'. On her third day she attended her first team meeting.

Jenny was very surprised to find that this meeting was not chaired by the team leader, but by a systems analyst. The team members contributed to the discussion without competing and complex decisions were taken quickly. Jenny's advice was sought straight away. What did the team have to do to ensure that the final system could easily be communicated to staff? What were likely to be the problems in setting up a training scheme?

Within a month Jenny had adapted to the team method of working and felt highly motivated. She felt part of a close-knit supportive group of people. Her opinions and expertise were valued by the other team members. She could see how her training area fitted into the whole scheme and she was proud at the praise given to her team by the chief executive on a visit.

Jenny's higher needs were being met in the team environment and so she was highly motivated.

One particular motivational problem with individual members of teams is their interaction with other team members. A team may have members who are particularly task oriented and not interested in 'people' aspects of work. They will not readily be motivated to cooperate with other members of the team on tasks not directly related to their own functional area (the engineer may find little interest in training). It will be necessary for the team leader to provide motivation in such cases by showing how each team member's specialist area is interdependent with the other specialist areas. The engineer needs to see that people will have to be trained to use the equipment, and that the equipment specification will be limited by the finances allocated.

SUMMARY

1. Many organisations now use teams as their preferred format for working.

2. Teams pose greater motivational problems than individuals in the normal line-management structure.

3. A team as a whole can be motivated in the same way as individuals. Primarily motivation comes through higher needs.

4. The team can be considered as being motivated in three areas:

❑ Task: the group's common achievement of their task.
❑ Group: the group's social needs.
❑ Individual: the individual needs of different group members.

5. Since the members of a team have to work as a team, all the members have to be motivated by being on the team. If this is not the case then they are unlikely to perform.

QUESTION

What are the differences in motivating individuals and individuals who are team members?

ANSWER

Individuals who are team members need to be motivated to work in the team. They may be task oriented and not people oriented but will still have to be motivated to contribute to the team's people areas.

10

MOTIVATING YOUR BOSS

Motivating your boss is as important as motivating your staff. Your boss is almost certainly partly responsible for your salary and promotion prospects, allocates work and can make your work easier or more difficult. If you can motivate your boss to make your work easier and your salary/promotion prospects better, it must be worthwhile!

How do you think you might do this?

I thought that your boss:

- [ ] will be motivated by praise – both from you and from others;
- [ ] needs to achieve and have self-fulfilment;
- [ ] needs to be part of a social group and to have social status;
- [ ] needs to take pride in her or his work;
- [ ] needs to be in control of the work for which he or she is responsible.

You probably thought of others.

How can you motivate your boss by helping him or her meet these needs? How can you ensure that your actions do not interfere with their meeting these needs?

Helping

You will motivate your boss by:

❑ Giving them praise for work they have done.
❑ Accepting them in your group at work.
❑ Feeding back information on work that you are doing so that they can monitor your progress and feel in control.
❑ Asking advice where they have greater knowledge, or where they wish to be asked for advice.
❑ Backing them in meetings and in conversations with other members of staff.
❑ Disagreeing, where you have to, in a calm, assertive but non-aggressive fashion.

Interfering

You will demotivate your boss by:

❑ Always criticising your boss's decisions, or never giving praise.
❑ Keeping apart from them at work so that they do not feel part of your group.
❑ Keeping your work to yourself and not reporting your progress.
❑ Appearing to know more than them and never asking advice.
❑ 'Running them down' behind their backs and not giving support at meetings.
❑ Arguing and disagreeing in an aggressive manner.

I am not suggesting that these are complete lists, but they indicate the main areas for your concentration.

CASE STUDY

I once had a boss who had a superb PA. She always completed projects on time, backed him both in public and in private and praised him when he achieved. He valued her greatly and made a moving speech praising her and acknowledging her help when she left the company. I met her a few months later, and she told me that she had disagreed with a lot of her boss's decisions but always discussed these with him in a nonthreatening way. She tried to make him see that she valued his experience but disagreed with his proposals. Sometimes she got him to change his mind, sometimes she didn't.

I had never realised that she disagreed with many of his decisions. She had always appeared totally loyal. When I thought about it, I realised that she had motivated him into making changes in many of his decisions. She could not have done this without her praise, loyalty and non-aggressive attitude. She was a very skilful motivator of her boss.

DIFFICULT BOSSES

Not all bosses are perfect. Some may have a small fault or two! What can you think of as main problems?

I thought of:

❑ aggressive and bad-tempered bosses;
❑ indecisive and inconsistent bosses;
❑ bosses who don't give recognition and praise;
❑ bosses who can't delegate, and interfere;
❑ bosses who don't keep you informed;
❑ bosses who can't cope with their job.

Note the similarity to the list in Chapter 4.

AGGRESSIVE AND BAD-TEMPERED

In the ideal world everyone would be assertive and not aggressive. Unfortunately a lot of senior people feel that they can get away with aggression – indeed they think that it 'keeps people in their place' and 'shows who's boss'! I have had several bosses like this.

If a boss is permanently bad-tempered and aggressive with everyone, there is probably very little that can be done. Most aggression, is however, occasional. In this case the best method is to bring the problem into the open in a non-aggressive way and point out the disadvantages. You might say: 'I have a problem and wonder if you could help me with it. When you get angry with me I find it upsetting, and it affects my work. If you could explain why I make you angry then I could try and adjust my behaviour.'

Usually bosses are surprised at this. They do not realise that they regularly get angry, nor that their anger affects others so strongly. In most cases there will be a temporary, reduction in aggression. When this happens you can reward it with praise by saying such things as: 'It's been great working for you today, I have felt really happy because you have been so pleasant – thank you!'

This may sound strange, but it usually works! It is called 'feedback technique'.[29] What doesn't work is getting angry yourself, or making a formal threatening complaint.

INDECISIVE AND INCONSISTENT

Here you can use feedback technique to motivate by rewarding decisiveness and consistency and by pointing out problems that are being caused by the opposite.

When you are given no clear decision, or a decision is altered several times, you can say something along the lines of: 'I'm not quite clear what you want here, and I don't want to do the wrong thing. Could you be a little more precise so that I can ensure that I do what you really want?' And when there has been decisive behaviour: 'Thanks, that was really clear and helpful, I can see exactly what you want done.'

Your boss will be motivated by the praise that you are giving – and also by the fact that the required task will be done correctly! You will also find it helpful to do the following:

❏ Repeat back instructions to make sure your boss is aware of what has been requested.
❏ Write down instructions. If these are changed, show surprise, bring out the list and alter it.

These two steps will make bosses aware of their indecision.

NOT GIVING RECOGNITION AND PRAISE

If you are never given recognition or praise, then you have a problem! You can only ask: 'You never seem to give me any praise, am I performing properly or are you dissatisfied?'

Hopefully there will be some occasions when you get recognition and praise. You can then use the feedback technique: 'Thank you, that really made me feel good. When you give me recognition I feel that working for you is a real pleasure and I feel motivated to work harder.'

You will have gathered by now that the main method of motivating your boss is by using the feedback technique to reward the behaviour that you want. You also, in most cases, need to outline the problem that the wrong behaviour is causing. This is a modification of the technique for motivating difficult employees outlined in Chapter 8. You will probably not want to use the exact words suggested here, but use words that feel comfortable to you.

REFUSAL TO DELEGATE

Having read this chapter so far, how would you going about dealing with the boss that will not delegate?

I hope that you would have used the technique of feedback, coupled with stating the problem. This may sound too simple, but it usually works!

It would be suitable to state the problem: 'I find it very difficult to do this job when I do not have the authority delegated to me. If you delegated to me I would ensure that I reported regularly to you to keep you in touch.'

And when delegation does take place: 'It was very helpful that you delegated to me, thank you. It made my job much easier.'

It would also be useful to find out why your boss does not delegate, and deal with the reason. For example your boss may be afraid that subordinates would make mistakes. In this case you could add to the first statement above: 'I realise that you may be worried that I may make a mistake. Perhaps we could go over your areas for concern and see what you would require to reassure you?'

You need to bring out the problem into the open and discuss it. This will go a long way towards resolving matters. Of course if your boss never delegates under any circumstances, then you may be better off finding another job!

Where your boss interferes, you will again need to point out the problem: 'It is difficult to carry out my work when you obviously want to do it rather than leave it to me.'

It will be difficult to motivate through feedback as you can hardly say 'thank you for not interfering'.

You might try: 'It was good of you to give me the chance to show that I could do this myself'.

NOT KEEPING YOU INFORMED

In this instance you need to be able to specify the problems caused by the lack of information. You need to convince your boss that it is in her or his interest to keep you informed. You will motivate them into informing you if they can see that by doing this your performance will improve.

You could say: 'I found it difficult to do X without full information. If I had the full information the job would have been done better.'

Or if you have not been given a piece of news, think of something dependent on it: 'I'm sorry that you did not tell me about X – it would have helped me when dealing with Y'.

Praise occasions when information is given: 'Thank you for letting me know about X, it was a great help, thank you.'

BOSSES WHO CAN'T COPE

This is a common problem. Often a boss has been promoted one step too far, or is out of touch with new technology. Such people will realise their inadequacy and will be very defensive. This may take the form of aggression, refusal to delegate, criticising subordinates, etc. In this instance it is not going to help if you bring matters out into the open – you will merely demotivate them by hurting their pride!

You will need to spot the specific areas where they are deficient, and specifically offer help in an unobtrusive way. This should not be in the form of 'shall I show you how to . . .' or 'would you like some help with . . .' but rather: 'I'm not sure how best we should do X and wondered if we could discuss it, it would help me a great deal.'

In both cases you will be able to help and also discuss the matter so that your boss feels that he or she has an input. In time your boss will be motivated to delegate more tasks to you. It will be obvious that you will not threaten them by exposing their shortcomings, but will rather satisfy their needs for achievement.

SUMMARY

In general you motivate your boss by ensuring that what you do is in their interests so that you are satisfying their need to achieve. You outline problem areas so that they can be brought out into the open, and reward the required behaviour by praise. Even a boss finds praise motivating!

QUESTION

Think of your boss. In what ways could you motivate him or her? Are there any problem areas?

Only you can provide the answer!

11

MOTIVATING YOURSELF

As you will have gathered from this book so far, you have to do most of the motivating of others.

But who or what motivates you?

Perhaps you would like to make a list of all the things and people that motivate you.

I expect that you had quite a big list! Next separate your list into the following headings:

❑ People who motivate you.
❑ Aspects of your organisation that motivate you.
❑ Parts of your job that motivate you (task-oriented motivation).
❑ Aspects of relationships with other people that motivate you (people-oriented motivation).
❑ Areas where you motivate yourself without any of the above (self-motivation).

This list will tell you several things:

❑ Whether you are being motivated by your boss and organisation or by others inside your organisation. If you are being motivated by others, what are the reasons for this?
❑ whether your motivation is primarily task or people oriented.
❑ the extent to which you are self-motivated (many people find they have little to list under self-motivation).

If you are finding little motivation from your boss and organisation then this is likely to be primarily their fault. You will need to identify the problem to your boss, indicating where she or hecould do things that would motivate you. You should use the technique from Chapter 9 – indicate then reinforce with praise.

Can you identify some areas where you feel that you could be motivated by your boss?

CASE STUDY

Mary was secretary to a marketing director, Sam. He was always very busy and left her tapes of dictation when he went away. When he came back, Mary had his letters ready. There were very rarely any mistakes. Sam simply signed the letters and gave them back to her without comment. Mary felt very demotivated. She had taken great care to ensure that the letters were perfect – but Sam never gave her any credit.

Mary decided to try and change things. The next time Sam handed her the letters back without comment she said, 'Were you dissatisfied with the letters Sam?' 'No they were fine – why?' replied Sam. 'Well, since you never comment on the letters, I assumed you were dissatisfied with my work.'

Sam was very surprised and said that he was very happy with the work Mary did. Mary then explained that she would appreciate it if Sam told her when he was happy with her work, and when he wasn't. This would enable her to ensure that she did the work as Sam wanted. Whenever Sam praised her work Mary said 'Thank you Sam, I appreciate that.'

Soon Sam regularly commented on Mary's work – mostly complimentary comments. Mary had motivated Sam to give her the encouragement that she needed for her own motivation.

Helping your boss to the right attitude towards you can greatly increase your own motivation. You also have the power to increase your own motivation. How do you do this?

The steps to increasing your own motivation are:

❑ Realising your own worth.
❑ Realising that you can change things.
❑ Thinking positively.
❑ Setting your goals.

REALISING YOUR WORTH

Write a five line description of yourself, emphasising your good points.

Most people find this surprisingly difficult! Our culture and upbringing teach us to be modest – we don't like blowing our own trumpet! Let's be a little more specific. Can you list ten things that you do well; or are good points about your character; or are things that you know other people like you for, or admire in you.

Make sure you spend time to get all ten!

I hope you tried really hard and got to ten! So you do have a lot of good attributes. You have worth. That means you are worth employing and worth rewarding. Self-motivation starts with a self-evaluation and realisiation of self-worth. Without our own realisation of our self-worth, and an ability to motivate ourselves, we cannot hope to motivate others.

If you have really had a problem listing ten good points and only listed two or three, then you do not realise your own worth. You might like to try the three-point diary method.[30] Record each day in a small pocket diary that you carry with you, three events that you really enjoyed (many of which will be things that you are good at). You will find that within a few days you will have started to identify things that you are good at. After a week you should go back and try listing the ten points above again. This time you will find that you have a lot more!

REALISING THAT YOU CAN CHANGE THINGS

You have control over your life! You can change it. You can change the way that you think about yourself. You can change the way that you live. You can change the way that you work. You may not *want* to change. You may prefer to live in your present 'contentment' zone. But you can change things.

CASE STUDY

Ten years ago I was 44 and a buyer for a supermarket chain. For a long time I had wanted to teach and write. At the time of writing I am 54, a tutor for the Open University Business School and have had four books on management published here and in the US. I am an External Fellow of the Faculty of Management of the University of Luton and am involved in education projects in the Middle East.

I decided to change things – so can you! You just have to want change, and realise that you do have the power to make the change.

THINKING POSITIVELY

Young children rarely think that they will fail at something. Failure is largely an adult concept, something we learn (often from experience) between the age of 6 and 12. Adults who try to learn to ski or water ski often find it very difficult. They know the difficulties. Although I learnt to mono water ski when I was 40, it took me over 20 attempts! Young children of around 6 or 7 have no problems at all learning to ski or water ski – they do not see the problems, they have faith in their abilities.

If we learn to think positively rather than negatively about our future, then we can change our futures.

❑ Step 1: want to change.
❑ Step 2: think positively that you can change.

How do you think positively? You first start by believing that things can change.

What would you like to change? What elements in your work and private life would you like to change? Write them down.

Now think of the barriers to these changes and write them down.

Do you really think that these barriers are insurmountable, that you can never make these changes?

CASE STUDY

I recently saw a television documentary about a woman who had been a down-and-out alcoholic drug addict for most of her life. She suddenly decided that she could change her life. She rehabilitated herself from drugs and alcohol, took a Master's Degree and is now studying for a Ph.D.

The Open University has many students who, starting with no academic qualifications at all, have achieved degrees. Quite a few are in their 80s. They wanted change and thought positively about it.

There are no real reasons why you cannot overcome your barriers, and change.

SETTING YOUR GOALS

If you are going to be able to change, you must first clearly set your goals.

Step 1: want to change.
Step 2: think positively that you can change.
Step 3: set your goals.

CASE STUDY

I said earlier that ten years ago I was in a situation where I had always wanted to write and teach – but was in commerce. I decided to set specific goals:

- ❏ I would retire from commerce by the time I was 55.
- ❏ I would try to obtain a little part-time teaching with the goal of having a proper part-time teaching job when I retired.
- ❏ I would try to write a little with the goal of being an established writer when I retired.

I enrolled on a correspondence writing course (yes, they do work!), had a couple of magazine articles published and was then asked to write a book. I applied to become a tutor for the Open University on a part-time basis – and was accepted. I started paying extra into my pension scheme to enable me to retire by 55.

Having set my goals I then put into motion the actions to help me achieve them. I have now achieved the goals that I set out ten years ago. There is no reason at all why you can't do the same.

Why am I bringing all this up in this chapter on self-motivation? It is because if you have decided on your future, and how to get there, you will be highly motivated. You will have planned ways to meet your higher needs of achievement and self-fulfilment. If you are highly motivated, you will find it much easier to motivate others. Motivation is infectious!

Once you have decided on your goals, and methods of achieving them – set a time scale. Tell yourself that you will achieve your goals by this date. As time goes by, check your progress. Remind yourself of your goals. My time-scale was a long one, ten years. Yours may be much shorter, but you will still need to check progress.

SUMMARY

The steps to increasing your own motivation are:

❑ Realising your own worth.
❑ Realising that you can change things.
❑ Thinking positively about your ability to change things.
❑ Setting your goals very specifically within a time-scale.

You have looked at what you want to change, and the barriers to this change.
   You should now:

❑ Set specific goals.
❑ Decide on means to achieve them.
❑ Set a time-scale.

Do not hurry this process. It may take a few days but will be time well spent. With your goals in front of you, you will be highly motivated. Remember motivation is infectious! You will become a better motivator.

12

A SUMMARY

A successful manager *motivates* people to produce the required results on time, and within budget. Motivation is the force that drives people to do things. People are usually motivated to satisfy *needs*.

Needs can be:

- ❑ *low level*: food, clothing, housing;
- ❑ *middle level*: a secure job, reasonable working conditions, reasonable pay;
- ❑ *high level*: the need to belong, to be in control, self-fulfilment, self-development, pride, etc.

Low-level needs are normally met in our society.

Middle-level needs only need to be satisfied. The 'satisfiers' (a secure job) etc will not provide more motivation if increased, but they will produce demotivation if reduced below the satisfactory level. If reduced below this satisfactory level, then people may leave the organisation.

Higher-level needs are the main motivators.

'Expectancy theory' lies behind a lot of motivation theory. This is

Performance → Reward or Punishment

Someone will be motivated if they can *expect* that a particular performance will always produce a reward or punishment.

You can use *trust and responsibility* to motivate your staff – they are powerful motivators. *Feedback* is also a powerful motivator, and *praise* is the most powerful form of feedback.

Strong motivational tools available to a manager include *goal setting, incentives, training: coaching/mentoring, appraisals*. These work as motivators through satisfying higher level needs for self fulfilment and pride.

Employees will only be motivated where they can see that the end product will be something that is to their own benefit.

The main leadership styles are:

❑ Autocratic: where the leader decides.
❑ Democratic: where decisions are reached by the group after discussion.
❑ Consultative: where the leader consults staff and then makes a decision.

If you take autocratic as one end of a scale, and democratic at the other, there are many positions in between that can be valid leadership styles. The style most appropriate to any situation will depend on the situation.

Staff will be motivated if you choose the appropriate leadership style for the situation. Most situations require consultative leadership but there will always be occasions requiring autocratic and democratic styles. Only the correct leadership style for the situation will produce full motivation.

People want to work for reasons connected with three main areas of needs:

❑ people related;
❑ task related;
❑ self-awareness/self-development.

This assumes that their basic requirement for an acceptable wage has been met. By identifying one or more of these areas as the main reason for someone wanting to work, you will be able to work out the best means of providing motivation. You can best identify the areas during a formal discussion such as an appraisal, or by asking yourself a series of questions about that person.

In general when dealing with 'problem people':

❑ identify the problem;
❑ decide on the best method to minimise or eliminate the problem;
❑ decide on the best method to motivate by identifying the needs that you can meet.

Many organisations now use teams as their preferred format for working. Teams pose greater motivational problems than individuals in the normal line-management structure. A team as a whole can be motivated in the same way as individuals. Primarily motivation comes through higher needs.
   A team can be considered as being motivated in three areas:

❑ Task: the group's common achievement of their task.
❑ Group: the group's social needs.
❑ Individual: the individual needs of group members.

In general you motivate your boss by ensuring that what you do is in their interests so that you are satisfying their need to achieve. You outline problem areas so that they can be brought out into the open, and reward the required behaviour by *feedback* and *praise*. Even a boss finds praise motivating!
   The steps to increasing your own motivation are:

❑ Realising your own worth.
❑ Realising that you can change things.
❑ Thinking positively about your ability to change things.
❑ Setting your goals very specifically with a time scale.

Motivation is infectious!

A CHECKLIST FOR MOTIVATION

First of all – is your organisation or department motivated? Think again about the checklist in Chapter 2.

	Employees are happy		Employees are unhappy
	Employees are cooperative		Employees do not cooperate
	Employees accept responsibility for their work		Employees blame others for mistakes
	Employees rarely off work		Employees often absent
	Output always high		Output below targets
	Quality high		Quality often below target
	Tasks completed on time		Tasks often late
	Management is respected		Employees complain about management

If you have any ticks at all in the right-hand column, then you probably have motivation problems. If you have no ticks in the right-hand column you probably have no major motivational problems but can probably improve performance by improving motivation still further.

Now make a list of the staff directly responsible to you. Think about each one and their motivation for working. Would you class them as task oriented, people oriented or self-fulfilment oriented?

On the next page we have an individual motivation plan. You may like to photocopy one for each member of staff. Prepare your individual motivation plans using the methods you have learnt in this book – summarised above.

MOTIVATION PLAN

Name . . . .

Job Description

Can this job be altered to provide greater motivation?

Motivational type (Task, people, self-fulfilment) . . . .

Any identified problems

Have I had a discussion/appraisal to determine the above, or is it based on observation?

If I have not had a personal discussion/ appraisal, when might I be able to do this?

Proposed dates for review of progress . . . .
(suggested monthly intervals)

Review 1 Comments

Review 2 Comments

Review 3 Comments

Review 4 Comments

REFERENCES

1. Taylor, F W (1911) *Principles of Scientific Management*, Harper & Row, New York.
2. Drucker, P F (1974) *Management: Tasks, Responsibilities, Practices*, Harper & Row, New York.
   Herzberg, F (1959) *The Motivation to Work*, Wiley, New York.
   Maslow, A H (1970) *Motivation and Personality*, Harper & Row, New York.
3. Vroom, V H (1964) *Work and Motivation*, Wiley, New York.
4. Mayo, E (1933) *The Human Problems of an Industrial Civilisation*, Macmillan, London.
5. Herzberg, F (1959) *The Motivation to Work*, Wiley, New York.
6. Kahn, R L (1958) article in *Human Relations and Modern Management*, Amsterdam.
7. Paul, W J and Robertson, K B (1970) *Job Enrichment and Employee Motivation*, Gower, London.
8. Hackman, J R and Oldham, G R (1976) 'Motivation Through Design of Work', published in *Organizational Behaviour and Human Performance*, 16, pp 250–79.
9. Porter, L W and Lawler, E E (1968) *Managerial Attitudes and Performance*, Harvard University, Boston, Mass.
10. Harvey, C (1992) *Successful Motivation in a Week*, Headway, London.
11. Luhn, R H (1992) *Managing Anger*, Kogan Page, London.

12. Skinner, B F (1973) *Beyond Freedom and Dignity*, Penguin, London.
13. Locke, E A (1976) 'The Nature and Causes of Job Satisfaction', in *The Handbook of Industrial and Organizational Psychology*, Rand McNally, Chicago, Ill.
14. O'Conner, J and Seymour, J (1994) *Training with NLP*, Thorsons, London.
15. Maddux, R B (1986) *Effective Performance Appraisals*, Kogan Page, London.
16. Ibid.
17. White, R and Lippit, R (1983) in *Group Dynamics* (ed) Cartwright and Zander.
18. Tannenbaum, R and Schmidt, W (1958) in *Harvard Business Review*, March/April, Harvard University, Boston, Mass.
19. Adair, J (1983) *Effective Leadership*, Gower, London.
20. Luthens, F and Kreitner, R (1975) *Organizational Behaviour Modification*, Scott, Foresman & Co, Glenview, Ill. Payne, R (1984) 'Organizational Behaviour' in (ed) Cooper, C L and Makin, P, *Psychology for Managers*, Macmillan, London.
21. Fiedler, F E (1976) *A Theory of Leadership Effectiveness*, McGraw Hill, New York.
    Gowler, D and Legge, K (1980) 'Evaluative Practices as Stressors', in *Current Concerns in Occupational Stress*, Wiley, Chichester.
22. Mackenzie Davey, D (1989) *How to be a Good Judge of Character*, Kogan Page, London.
23. Aiken, L R (1988) *Psychological Testing and Assessment*, Allyn and Bacon, Boston.
    Holdsworth, R F (1972) *Personnel Selection and Testing: A Guide for Managers*, British Institute of Management, London.
    Toplis, J, Dulewicz, V and Fletcher, C (1991) *Psychological Testing: A Guide for Managers*, Institute of Personnel Management, London.
24. Cava, R (1990) *Dealing with Difficult People*, Piatkus, London.
    Wylie, P and Grothe, M (1993) *Problem Employees*, Piatkus, London.

25. Cooper, C L and Makin, P (1981) *Psychology for Managers*, Macmillan, London.
26. Skinner, B F (1976) *About Behaviourism*, Vintage Books, New York.
27. Allan, J S (1994) *25 Team Management Training Sessions*, Gower, London.
28. Adair, J (1985) *Effective Team Building*, Gower, London.
29. Cava, R (1990) *Dealing with Difficult People*, Piatkus, London.
30. Harvey, C (1992) *Successful Motivation in a Week*, Headway, London.

INDEX